Goddesses in You

Christine Lister is a wise woman, an elder and an old soul. Also, a goddess in many guises. Using moon goddess symbolism, which echoes the rhythms of nature, she is in the winter of her life and the new moon phase. A time of new beginnings and rebirth. For Christine, this is the perfect time to share the myths that have become her reality, her truths, in the hope that you too may discover the goddesses in you.

Goddesses in You

Discovering the myths and
archetypes that are your reality

CHRISTINE LISTER

First published 2022

Exisle Publishing Pty Ltd
PO Box 864, Chatswood, NSW 2057, Australia
226 High Street, Dunedin, 9016, New Zealand
www.exislepublishing.com

A CiP record for this book is available from the National Library of Australia.

ISBN 978-1-922539-34-2

Designed by Enni Tuomisalo

Typeset in PT Serif, 10pt

Printed in China

This book uses paper sourced under ISO 14001 guidelines from well-managed forests and other controlled sources.

10 9 8 7 6 5 4 3 2 1

Disclaimer

While this book is intended as a general information resource and all care has been taken in compiling the contents, neither the author nor the publisher and their distributors can be held responsible for any loss, claim or action that may arise from reliance on the information contained in this book. As each person and situation is unique, it is the responsibility of the reader to consult a qualified professional regarding their personal circumstances.

For the Goddess Kimmy Murray

A precious friend in a divine class of her own

Contents

Preface

The universe guides us in oft
mysterious and magical ways.

My fascination with Goddesses began in 2013 when I was working on a book. It was about a widowed writer letting go of the past, awakening to life and living again by opening up her world, reconnecting with the beauty of life and the possibility that love could still be there.

In response to my writing, a friend sent me an image of a ceramic tile by Sir Arthur Boyd — *Woman Lying in a Field*. It was an epiphany. I was entranced. This divine woman captured my heart and my imagination. I wanted to become a Goddess, too. And so, the memoir pivoted to become a sacred rite of passage from widow to woman to Goddess.

With each revelatory experience, a new Goddess emerged — the Goddess of the Moon, the Goddess of Earth. By the time the third Goddess, the Goddess of the Dawn, appeared, I decided to commission a talented young painter to give form to my words, to bring my Goddesses into being. By 2015, eight portraits of the Goddesses in me were beckoning me to look deeper.

Research, starting with the classic *Goddesses in Everywoman: Powerful archetypes in women's lives*, was a revelation; I devoured this and Jean Shinoda Bolen's books. Then further readings about Goddesses, mythology, spirituality, feminism and archetypes, which brought me to other classics now indelibly etched in my mind: *Women Who Run with the Wolves: Myths and stories of the wild woman archetype* by Clarissa Pinkola Estés; Joseph Campbell's work on mythology, particularly *The Hero's Journey*. Then onto Caroline Myss — *Anatomy of the Spirit*, *Archetypes* and *Sacred Contracts*, before returning to Swiss psychiatrist and psychologist Carl Jung's seminal work on the unconscious mind and archetypes and his autobiography, *Memories, Dreams, Reflections*.

> I can understand myself only in the light of inner happenings.
> —Carl Jung, *Memories, Dreams, Reflections*

Psychology coalesced with mythology, spirituality, feminism and my women's wisdom. But I needed four more Goddesses to span the panorama of the twelve major feminine archetypes in me — the most powerful influences in my life, the underlying unconscious archetypal behavioural traits, the DNA that shaped me. And, I realized, shape the roles of most contemporary women at some stage in their lives.

Now in 2022, thirteen Goddess portraits adorn my bedroom walls — the original inspiration, and twelve Greco-Roman Goddesses. The time has now come for me to share these divine feminine deities, the mythology of each Goddess, the type of Goddess, the feminine archetypes associated with them, plus real-life examples of how the Goddess is expressed in others. And I trust that you, too, will be inspired to discover the Goddesses in you.

Introduction

Archetypal patterns are like the door into a hidden realm, a parallel reality ... [They] hold the key to the real you.

—Caroline Myss, *Archetypes*

» Who are you?

» What makes up your personality?

» At the deepest level, what instinctively drives you?

» What stereotypical gender roles are expected of you?

» Are you living the life of your true self?

A Goddess is a divine being embodied in a feminine form, often with supernatural powers or attributes. Goddesses are often associated with virtues such as love, marriage, motherhood, fertility, wisdom or freedom. Ancient peoples in various civilizations and religions worshipped the Goddess in her many forms. However, the simplest manifestation of the Goddess was as Mother Earth. The Earth is the giver of life; the Earth nurtures and sustains life, and so can be likened to the powers of a woman — that of being the womb of creation, the supreme feminine creator.

Myths are sacred traditional tales that explain the world and our shared human experience: stories with universal truths and wisdoms embedded in them. Myths answer timeless questions and remain as relevant today as they were to ancient civilizations. They are expressions of archetypes and archetypal patterns in which we instinctively know how the story goes: happy, sad; tragedy, triumph; love, romance, heartbreak; damnation, redemption. In the same way, we instinctively know our own stories. By interpreting them, intellectually or intuitively, we bring out their symbolic meaning, as we do with dreams.

Archetypes are like the DNA code for all humankind. They contain universal themes of human life, inborn models of people or personalities that play a role in shaping human behaviour. The concept of archetypes was introduced by Carl Jung, who suggested that they were archaic forms of innate human knowledge passed down from our ancestors, largely based on mythological figures. He described these archetypes as symbols of basic human motivations that drive our desires and goals, and which become personalized when they are part of our own psyche.

> An archetype is something like an old watercourse along which the water of life flowed for a time, digging a deep channel for itself. The longer it flowed the deeper the channel, and the more likely it is that sooner or later the water will return.
> —Carl Jung, *Collected Works Volume 10: Civilization in Transition*

> Each goddess archetype possesses both positive and
> negative traits — they represent the light and the shadow
> sides of human consciousness ... Since we all embody the
> light and the dark, we can't have one without the other.
>
> —Sara Daves, *Goddess Archetypes*

The shadow can be described as the darker side of the psyche, representing wildness, chaos and the unknown. It is part of the unconscious mind and comprises repressed ideas, weaknesses, desires, instincts and shortcomings. The shadow is often formed from our attempts to adapt to cultural norms and expectations, and contains everything that is unacceptable not only to society but also to one's own personal morals and values.

The development of sex roles and gender identities is influenced by physiological changes as well as the social context. In many cultures, men and women are expected to adopt traditional and often stereotypical gender roles, and are discouraged from exploring aspects of their opposite gender. This, Jung believed, served to undermine psychological development.

Archetypes are a mirror into yourself, a psychic lens into your soul. The more you learn about the nature of an archetype, the more you understand yourself. The number of existing archetypes in you is not static or fixed. There are natal archetypes, ones that travel with us from birth to death. Then there are other archetypes we visit now and again but which are not enduring.

Activation of a specific archetype of the Goddess in you is influenced by both inner and outer forces — by your innate predisposition; by your parents' expectations of you; the era you live in; the culture you live in; the cultural stereotypes imposed on you; the phase of your life (puberty, menstruation, pregnancy, menopause); other people, events and experiences; and your spiritual practices and lifestyle. Archetypes are also contextual: if your life situation changes, a different archetype may be activated.

> There are goddesses in everywoman.
>
> —Jean Shinoda Bolen, *Goddesses in Everywoman*

Connecting with your Goddess is the key to finding your true self. A woman may go through long phases in her life where she embodies only one Goddess. More often, she will embody several Goddesses at any given time. They may overlap or combine; they may manifest continuously throughout her life or come and go; but typically, she will be drawn to those Goddess archetypes that best reflect her inherent energy and personality.

Using an intuitive blend of mythology, psychology, feminism, spirituality and women's wisdom, this book introduces you to twelve Goddesses, each of whom relates to a feminine archetype, or archetypes. Together, they create the panorama of attributes and the fullness of the feminine nature that exists in human imagination and the collective unconscious (the common collective memory).

Exploring the profiles of 60 notable women, we will see how these underlying unconscious archetypal behavioural traits are the powerful invisible threads, the DNA, that shape the roles and govern the beliefs, deepest desires, drives, motivations, actions and emotions of most women.

Discovering how these mythological Goddesses from a patriarchal past and how their feminine archetypes shape behaviour and personality traits, influence emotions and relationships, and are responsible for the major differences in women, can awaken us to a new way of seeing ourselves and lead to a better understanding of those around us. The truth is, every woman is a Goddess and therefore innately divine.

> There's nothing you can do that's more important than being fulfilled. You become a sign, you become a signal, transparent to transcendence; in this way, you will find, live, and become a realization of your own personal myth.
> —Joseph Campbell, *Pathways to Bliss*

Introducing the twelve Greco-Roman Goddesses

On the following page, I list the twelve Greco-Roman Goddesses and the domains they preside over. For the first eleven Goddesses, the first name given is the Greek name, with the Roman equivalent in brackets. This is reversed for the Goddess of Freedom as the Greek Goddess of Freedom was not always recognized as a Goddess in her own right.

Gaia (Terra)	Goddess of Earth
Selene (Luna)	Goddess of the Moon
Eos (Aurora)	Goddess of the Dawn
Artemis (Diana)	Goddess of the Hunt and the Moon
Athena (Minerva)	Goddess of Wisdom, War and Crafts
Hestia (Vesta)	Goddess of the Hearth, Home and Hospitality
Hera (Juno)	Goddess of Marriage, Queen of the Gods
Demeter (Ceres)	Goddess of the Grain, Harvest and Fertility
Persephone (Proserpina)	Goddess of Spring, Queen of the Underworld
Aphrodite (Venus)	Goddess of Love, Beauty and Desire
Psyche (Psyche)	Goddess of the Soul
Libertas (Eleutheria)	Goddess of Freedom

These twelve Goddesses can be classified into four categories: elemental, independent, relational and transformational.

Elemental Goddesses

Embedded in many ancient and magical traditions, the elemental Goddesses are related to, and embody, the powers of nature, with the world viewed as being formed from a mix of these elemental forces. As Goddesses reflect aspects of the natural world, many appear as the personification of these elements.

The elemental Goddesses are responsible for the conservation of nature and humanity, with characteristics representing the various elements and concepts such as Earth, air, fire, water, light, sky and spirit. Or any other naturally occurring phenomena such as the sun, moon and stars, trees and mountains. Elemental Goddesses are attuned to the elements, the seasons, the tides and the natural rhythms of Mother Nature herself. Aspects of the elemental Goddesses can be found in all women.

One of the primordial elemental deities, *Gaia, Goddess of Earth* is the great mother of all creation. The Earth Mother archetype represents balance and harmony on the Earth, wholeness in the universe, and is symbolic of fertility and abundance on the planet.

Selene, Goddess of the Moon forms a central role in mythology. The moon is associated with the divine feminine, and was important in ancient calendars, fertility, navigating the land and seas, and moon magic.

The four main Lunar Feminine archetypes we can cycle through during our lives — Maiden, Mother, Enchantress and Crone or Wise Woman — are all connected to a different season, a different phase of the moon and a different phase of the menstrual cycle.

Eos, Goddess of the Dawn rose from her home, near the river Oceanus, into the sky at the start of each day, dispersing the night. She symbolizes rebirth.

The Solar Feminine is a creative, passionate and radiant feminine energy, fuelled by compassion and purpose. The Solar Feminine is not one archetype. It can be found in vision, power, achievement and artistic expression.

Independent Goddesses

Independent Goddesses, or virgin Goddesses as they were known in ancient Greece, were free, sexually independent and not answerable to anyone. They represent self-sufficiency and autonomy in the female psyche. Relationship-independent, they do not need a partner or to be validated by a partner. They exist in their own right.

Independent Goddesses are goal-oriented and focus on activity, creativity, purpose and success, on what is important to them. Independent Goddesses are logical thinkers, open to the world but also in touch with their inner world and spirituality. They have a tendency to become totally absorbed in what matters to them.

The challenge for independent Goddesses is to avoid fulfilling traditional women's roles and remain true to themselves, and to find ways to adapt to living in patriarchal societies.

Artemis, the Goddess of the Hunt and the Moon felt a sisterly bond with other women, a spiritual bond with nature, and was very competitive. She avoided contact with men and spent her time in the wilderness with her band of nymphs. Artemis is the personification of the wild, free, female spirit.

Athena, the Goddess of Wisdom, War and Crafts was a tactician, warrior, craftswoman and a wise woman. Athena identified with men and joined them as an equal or superior.

Hestia, Goddess of the Hearth, Home and Hospitality was the keeper of the flame and the caretaker of the home, where the home is perceived as a temple. She was an introvert, focused on her inner spiritual world, and preferred solitude.

Relational Goddesses

Relational Goddesses represent the traditional roles of women whose identity, sense of purpose, meaning and wellbeing depend on being in a significant relationship. They personify the archetypes of wife, mother and daughter, and express the needs of women and their specific archetype for connection — to mate, to nurture, or to be dependent.

But there is an inherent vulnerability in these roles because of their dependence on others to satisfy their needs. Every relational Goddess was victimized. They suffered infidelity, broken attachments, cruelty, rape, abduction, domination, humiliation and feelings of powerlessness. Relational Goddesses, therefore, are more prone to falling prey to their shadow sides.

Hera, the Goddess of Marriage and Queen of the Gods is the archetype of wife and queen, who is committed to her relationship and her desire to mate.

Demeter, the Goddess of the Grain, Harvest and Fertility is the archetypal caring mother, who has the desire to nurture and a compelling maternal instinct.

Persephone, the Goddess of Spring and Queen of the Underworld is the archetypal daughter, and holds the desire to be dependent. She symbolizes youth, innocence, vulnerability and a sexually unawakened woman.

Transformational Goddesses

Transformational Goddesses, or alchemical Goddesses as they are sometimes known, represent the archetypes of celebration, change, metamorphosis, passion and wholeness. They encourage us to surrender to the power of flow, to dance, let go and release.

Transformational Goddesses are worshipped for their beauty, their magnetic personalities and magical power to transform — themselves, others and even societies. They are driven souls with the energy and synergy to touch deep chords in themselves and others, which often results in the creation of something new.

Transformational Goddesses often believe in a dream and are dedicated to making it come true. But the road to fulfilment is never easy. Often it is dark, lonely and filled with Herculean challenges and stresses — physical, mental, emotional, social and spiritual, which may invoke their shadow side.

Aphrodite, the Goddess of Love, Beauty and Desire is the archetypal lover and creative. Her beauty and magnetic presence enticed mortals and deities to enter into illicit affairs or fall in love and conceive of new life. Aphrodite inspired poetry and art and symbolizes the transformative and creative power of love and sexuality.

Psyche, Goddess of the Soul was once a mortal princess whose beauty rivalled that of Aphrodite, inspiring Aphrodite to jealousy and a dastardly plan to get rid of her rival. Psyche's journey from mortal to Goddess and becoming the wife of Eros, is the journey of the archetypal heroine.

Libertas, the Goddess of Freedom symbolizes liberty, independence and freedom, both personal and societal. Libertas supported and promoted the freeing of slaves.

1

Gaia

Goddess
of Earth

Archetype: Earth Mother

Nature is our source. The trees are our lungs, the air is
our breath, the waters are our circulation and the Earth
is our body. All of us resonate with deep, all-knowing
wisdom, an ancient familiarity as we connect with the
source of life itself.

—Shikoba Wolfe

Gaia mythology

In Greek mythology, the first Goddess was Gaia, Goddess of Earth, the primeval mother. To the Romans she was Terra Mater. All life and all Gods emanated from Mother Earth's fertile womb, and unto her all living things will return.

The concept of the Great Mother, Earth Mother or Mother Nature existed in many cultures and traditions. Gaia symbolizes all life and fertility and is the personification of the seasons. She is often portrayed as a voluptuous woman, surrounded by fruit and rising from the rich earth, inseparable from her native element.

According to Hesiod, the ancient Greek poet, in the beginning there was only Chaos. No before, no concept of time, just Chaos — nebulous ethers waiting to take form. The primordial landscape awaited direction. Into this timeless void came Gaia (the Earth), Tartarus (the Underworld) and Eros (desire). Gaia conceived the Earth, spontaneously birthing all forms of landscapes, plants and creatures, as well as two sons — Uranus, the sky, and Pontos, the sea.

Simultaneously, the other primordial deities, the first entities or beings to come into existence, emerged. These twelve most basic elements of the universe materialized fully formed at the dawn of creation: Earth, air, sea, sky, fresh water, Underworld, darkness, night, light, day, procreation and time.

Gaia then needed to mate. Choosing her son, Uranus, as her husband, time and cosmic history began. From their fruitful union came twelve children — six males and six females. These heavenly Gods and Goddesses were destined to become the Second Order of divine beings, the legendary Titans, taller than the mountains they used as thrones. Gaia later remarried, and with her new husband (Pontos, her son) gave birth to the sea Gods. In this way, all the later pantheon of Gods and Goddesses descended from Gaia's unions with Uranus and Pontos.

Gaia was a fearless protagonist, especially when it came to protecting her children. First, she came into conflict with her husband Uranus, who had imprisoned her giant-sons within her womb. Then, when her son Cronus defied her by imprisoning these same sons, she sided with Zeus in his rebellion against the Titans. Finally, after Zeus had bound her Titan-sons in Tartarus, Gaia tried to overthrow him, using her other giant-sons and the monster Typhoeus, but failed in both attempts.

However, Gaia never lost her strength, authority and high status as Goddess of Earth and ancestress of all. She not only represents the ancient Greek Mother Earth and the physical planet, but she also represents the forces of nature: laws and intelligences that function on every level of the cosmos. Gaia is the very fabric of existence.

Gaia archetype: Earth Mother (Mother Nature)

The Earth Mother is an elemental archetype, a basic element of the universe that embodies the power of nature. She represents balance and harmony on the Earth and wholeness in the universe. The Earth Mother archetype is symbolic of fertility and abundance on the planet. Gaia, as Earth Mother, is responsible for bringing humanity into being.

Gaia personifies the entire ecosystem of planet Earth. The Earth Mother archetype is about survival and sustainability. Those who embody this archetype understand the part they play within the natural cycles of nature. The Earth Mother embodies nurturing, protection and care. This means care of offspring and all creatures, both real and metaphorical, care of environments, and vitally, care of oneself — nurturing body, mind and spirit, not as a luxury, but as a necessity.

The archetypal Earth Mother possesses many positive qualities. Her maternal and nurturing qualities, kindness and compassion make her an excellent source of succour, support and advice for those experiencing difficulties in the world. Her wisdom, emotional intelligence and knowledge gained through experience of the world gives her an intuitive sense of how best to act in any given situation. Earth Mother archetypes also have an innate sense of spirituality, are in touch with the less tangible and more unconscious aspects of the world in which they live, and guide others in these areas.

Gaia archetypes are often passionate and dedicated to the causes they believe in. They are driven by a strong sense of duty to protect and care for what they love and nurture, or that which is vulnerable. They are prepared to take a stand, publicly or privately. Whether for people, places or the planet.

Although the Gaia archetype is a feminine energy, Gaia is just as readily found in males as in females, with the behavioural traits likely to be apparent from early in life. Carl Jung suggested that the archetypal Earth Mother is part of the collective unconscious of all human beings; that Gaia — the nurturer, the healer, the giver of life, the giver of dreams — resides in all of us. Also, the connection to the Earth is an elemental one and therefore likely to be a dominant lifelong characteristic.

Gaia archetypes can also be found in artists, innovators, inventors, architects, musicians, writers and dreamers, creators focused on moving beyond the bounds of current realities and perceptions, with fresh visions of what could be. Making a difference to the worlds in which they will live.

Light: loving, nurturing, kind, compassionate, humane; wise, intuitive, spiritual, affinity with nature; passionate, dedicated, determined; visionary, dreamer, expansive, future-oriented; strong sense of duty of care and protection for whatever they believe in, willing to fight to preserve life or the planet

Shadow: can become so focused on the big picture that their own needs or the needs of those close to them are neglected; taking on too much, burnout; can be perceived as too idealistic, a radical, a troublemaker, a greenie or a brat; may be tempted by thinking the end always justifies the means

Gaia in others

First Nations people, Jane Goodall, Greta Thunberg, journalist Julia Baird and domestic violence campaigner Rosie Batty all embody the Earth Mother archetype. They share a strong sense of dedication, a heart and soul connection to their cause — to nurturing and protecting what is important to them and what they believe in. Often for Gaia archetypes, the stakes and the stress levels are sky high, and the darker side lurks in the shadows, seeking means of expression.

First Nations people

The greatest Australian cultural example of Gaia is the deep relationship between the nation's Indigenous people and the land, which is known as 'connection to country'. For them, the land is their mother, the giver of life who provides them with everything they need. The environment is at the heart of every aspect of their identity — physical, social, cultural and spiritual.

> If you can imagine the one family continuously
> occupying the same land for 40,000 years or more,
> using it not just to sustain life but as a place of reverence
> and worship, where every tree, rock and waterhole
> had significance, you will get some understanding
> of the importance of land to Indigenous people.
> —Tania Major, *Young Australian of the Year 2007*

Indigenous Australian lore differs from western or European law. Created during the Dreamtime, it guides the culture and customs of the Indigenous people, and varies from one tribe (also known as a nation) to the next. One overarching obligation is caring for country. This is based on a reciprocal relationship between individuals and their ancestral lands and seas that is based on respect. While the land sustains and provides for the people, people manage and sustain the land through care, culture and ceremony.

With the coming of Europeans, traditional British law was imposed on the Indigenous people. *Terra nullius* declared the land uninhabited, which led to the Indigenous people being dispossessed from their ancestral lands. The devastation caused by colonization, violence, loss of land, lore, language and culture, and policies such as the forced removal of Indigenous children from their families, cast a dark shadow over Australia's history and the lives of Indigenous Australians, and continues to have negative impacts.

Today, no matter where they live, Indigenous Australians respect the obligation to return home to country to renew family and spiritual ties.

> Forget about the colour of our skins and that. Forget about
> our different lifestyles and our different belief systems,
> but believe in one thing and believe in Mother Earth so
> that we can look after it because she's looking after us.
>
> —Max Dulumunmun Harrison (Uncle Max)

Jane Goodall (1934–)

Jane Goodall is an English primatologist. With 60 years of ground-breaking research to her credit, she is the world's leading authority on chimpanzees. Jane's fascination with wildlife was evident from early childhood, when she dreamt of living in Africa to watch and write about animals. At 23 she travelled to Kenya, the highlight being meeting famed anthropologist and palaeontologist, Dr Louis Leakey.

Soon after, Jane and Dr Leakey began a study, with Jane braving a world of unknowns to realize her childhood dream. 'I don't care two hoots for civilization,' she said, 'I want to wander in the wild.'

Although she knew very little about chimpanzees, Jane took an unorthodox approach to her research, becoming Mother Nature incarnate and immersing herself in their habitat in the forest of Gombe. In this way, Jane was able to observe and understand the behaviour of chimps first-hand — as a species and as individuals — and become, in her words, 'more in tune with the spiritual power I felt all around'.

At first, the animals fled when Jane entered the forest, but with patience and determination she searched the forest every day, deliberately avoiding getting too close to the chimpanzees too soon. Gradually, the chimpanzees accepted her presence, enabling her to discover secrets about how they lived, what they ate, how they made tools to forage; and that chimpanzees have emotions, minds, personalities and form long-term bonds. 'Chimps taught us we are not separated from the animal kingdom; we are part of it,' she has said.

After Gombe, the Gaia in Jane remained dedicated to her beloved chimpanzees, finding other powerful means to protect and nurture them. Jane went on to found the Jane Goodall Institute and several other initiatives, including Roots and Shoots, a youth service program, all to encourage wildlife conservation efforts.

Jane, the Earth Mother, believes, 'each one of us matters, has a role to play, and makes a difference. Each one of us must take responsibility for our own lives, and above all, show respect and love for living things around us, especially each other.'

Like Gaia, Jane is prepared to do anything and everything to protect chimps from exploitation and extinction, and is a fearless advocate for chimpanzees in captivity. When she began her work, chimps were routinely used in medical research, a practice she helped to stop in many countries. While in lockdown caused by the Covid-19 pandemic, the chimps remained uppermost in her mind. 'Being isolated has made me think of what it must be like for chimpanzees who were isolated in captivity, who depend on physical closeness and touch,' she commented.

Today, Jane travels the globe, devoting her time, skill and efforts to fundraising and continuing the research at her institute. A major focus is to create awareness of the urgent threats facing chimpanzees and the environment. Jane is a Goddess of the Earth dedicated to urging people everywhere to take action, to protect all living things and the planet.

> My mission is to create a world that
> is in harmony with nature.
> —Jane Goodall

Greta Thunberg (2003–)

Swedish environmental activist, Greta Thunberg, first learnt about the issue of climate change when she was eight years old, and found her mission in life soon after. The Gaia in her emerged, manifesting as a deep concern for the planet. She changed her own habits, becoming a vegan and refusing to travel by plane. Greta believed, 'You are never too small to make a difference.'

Seeking to make a greater impact, Greta attempted to spur lawmakers and leaders into addressing climate change. At fifteen, for almost three weeks prior to the Swedish election in 2018, she missed school to sit outside the country's parliament with a sign that stated, 'School strike for climate'.

Although alone for the first day of the strike, as her story gained international attention more and more people joined in, with hundreds of thousands of students around the world inspired to participate in their own Fridays for the Future. Greta was invited to speak about climate change at the World Economic Forum, the European Parliament and a UN climate event in New York, and was pleased with the outcome. 'We showed that we are united,' she commented, 'and that we, young people, are unstoppable.'

Greta is not content to merely raise awareness, preferring to stand up to powerful patriarchal interests. She challenged world leaders to stop talking and take immediate action: 'You have stolen my dreams and my childhood with your empty words ... People are suffering. People are dying. Entire ecosystems are collapsing. We are in the beginning of a mass extinction, and all you can talk about is money, and fairytales of eternal economic growth. How dare you!'

Some in the media have criticized and mocked her for having Asperger's syndrome. They see it as an unruly, shadow aspect of her personality. Speaking in *The Guardian,* Tony Attwood, a world authority on Asperger's, said people diagnosed are 'usually renowned for being direct, speaking their mind and being honest and determined and having a strong sense of social justice.' Greta acknowledges that her diagnosis has limited her before, noting that before she started campaigning she stayed home alone. Now, however, she sees being different from the norm as a superpower.

Like Gaia, Greta is a fearless protagonist, willing to fight for and protect what she believes in. Wise to the shadow aspects of her personality, she is also wise in the ways of the world and of strategy. This teenage Earth Mother knows how to mobilize the masses, use disruptive tactics, take on powerful vested political and financial interests, and change the narrative about the climate crisis.

Greta is a Goddess of Earth, committed to save the world from burning.

Julia Baird (1967–)

Everyone will, at some stage in their lives, encounter loss, grief, hardship, trauma or serious illness, and thus potentially experience fear or strong emotions, when the path ahead seems too hard, when the way of life is threatened, or when life itself is imperilled.

Like many people, Australian journalist, broadcaster and author Julia Baird discovered it is the time to tap into the spirit and strength of the ancient Earth Mother archetype; to connect with Gaia, the giver of life; to connect with the living environment and the elemental forces of nature.

How do we continue to glow when the lights turn out? That's the question Julia asked when a life-threatening condition and pain began to overwhelm her. The health-conscious mother of two children had often wondered how it might feel to have cancer growing inside her body, but after being diagnosed with a rare form of cancer, terror gripped her. 'It's a peculiar, lonely kind of impotence, a cancer diagnosis … Your world narrows to a slit when facing a diagnosis like that; suddenly very little matters.'

Julia underwent a number of extremely traumatic surgeries to remove a tumour the size of a basketball lodged in her abdomen. Her personal experience led to an inspiring book, *Phosphorescence: On awe, wonder and things that sustain you when the world goes dark*, an exploration of how, even when facing the greatest odds, we can find, nurture and carry our own inner living light, the phosphorescence that will sustain us even in our darkest times. How finding Gaia, and the light within, helped her stay alive and remain upright, even when lashed by doubt.

In her research for the book, Julia spoke to psychologists, scientists, doctors, poets, artists, family members and friends. She read widely, tried many things herself and was impressed to find an entire body of research devoted to the importance of being around living things. She realized this was an ancient wisdom passed down for millennia by Indigenous people, about listening to and caring for country. And about that connection to family and tribe that is pivotal to physical, social, cultural and spiritual life and wellbeing.

In her quest to find *the light within*, it was awe and wonder Julia kept returning to. To the astonishing colours and otherworldliness of cuttlefish; to a mesmerizing assortment of creatures that glow; to bathing in the quiet healing properties of nature; and to the quiet places of escape and refuge so many of us have.

Her description of ocean swimming gives us a glimpse of how the elemental power of the sea can sustain and enhance life. 'As your arms circle, swing and pull along the edge of a vast ocean,' she writes, 'your mind wanders, and you open yourself to awe, to the experience of seeing something astonishing, unfathomable or greater than yourself.'

The Earth Mother in Julia was convinced there are elemental things that can sustain you through difficult times, if only we know how to recognize them. And to recognize that nurturing relationships and every human experience of awe and wonder is good for us — good for our health, general wellbeing, resilience, ethics and spirit.

> We must love. And we must look outwards and upwards at all times, caring for others, seeking wonder and stalking awe, every day, to find the magic that will sustain us and fuel the light within — our own phosphorescence.
> —Julia Baird

Rosie Batty (1962–)

Rosie Batty is an English-born Australian domestic violence campaigner. Her role as a campaigner began early in 2014 when Rosie's only child, Luke, an effervescent eleven-year-old, was at cricket practice at a local sports oval. Although parents, children and Rosie were present, they were some distance away. Luke's father managed to isolate him in the cricket nets, strike him over the head with a cricket bat, then brutally stab him to death while he lay on the ground. Police later shot and killed his father.

Within 24 hours of losing the most important person in her life, Rosie was thrust into the media spotlight, bravely talking about the reality of domestic violence in society. She has been an ambassador ever since. She started the Luke Batty Foundation during the same month as the senseless loss of her son and was awarded Australian of the Year for 2015. Rosie dedicated the award to Luke, acknowledging that he was the reason she found her voice.

'Being an advocate, I've got nothing to lose because I've got nothing more to be frightened about,' she said. 'If I have made a small difference then Luke hasn't died in vain. I feel proud — it makes me feel I have purpose and meaning in my life.' Rosie put aside her own heartache and fear to champion the cause of domestic violence, hoping to protect vulnerable others in ways she wasn't able to protect her own son.

In her public life, Rosie always presented as a strong, forthright woman, even if frequently and understandably teary. She made a connection with people because she was authentic and understood that domestic violence is a great social leveller. It can happen to anyone, to any family, just as it had to hers.

After four gruelling and unrelenting years of putting others first, of advocacy, and of running the foundation, the shadow aspects of this Earth Mother were gaining momentum and threatening to topple this tower of strength. Rosie realized that her pace of work was unsustainable. There were times when she felt totally overwhelmed and exhausted, burnt out. And she needed time to grieve. So, she made the decision to step down from the foundation and continue her work in less public ways.

Now, after seven years without Luke, Rosie is no longer constantly weighed by sorrow. The Gaia within has returned, with nature bringing her some solace and gratitude and the wherewithal to write a book about hope. Rosie's enduring courage and resilience make it possible for her to contemplate a life and a future without Luke.

When a person's archetype and personality are closely aligned — that is, they are living their truth — their life takes on greater meaning and purpose, and their experiences can sometimes seem sacred.

Gaia is easier to recognize in extraordinary women, but she is all around us, manifested in myriad ways. The Goddess of Earth can be found among the people we meet in our everyday lives. Ordinary women living ordinary and sometimes extraordinary lives, yet each divine in their own right, as the Goddess is intrinsically interwoven with who they are, what they believe in and their dedication and determination to make a difference in the world.

For many, the Gaia within is manifested in their choice of profession — in the health and wellbeing fields, hands-on charitable organizations or human rights agencies, where the Goddess is actively engaged in caring for and protecting others, mind, body and soul. Gaia can also be found in those unsung heroes: the good neighbour, the good friend, the caring nurse, the good Samaritan.

For others, Gaia shows up in their passion for protecting animals and the environment and this sustains and motivates them. For them, it is rescuing wildlife, unwanted or mistreated pets, saving endangered species, the reef or rainforests, planting trees to create koala corridors, farmers turning to organic farming or sustainable methods of farming. At other times, Gaia could be in the background, such as in scientific research to improve the quality of human and animal life, or the environment.

But, overarching all this, Gaia and the human spirit are indelibly etched in nature. She is the very fabric of our existence.

> This is the core of our task: to respect and revere ourselves, and so bring about a world in which women are respected and revered, recognised once again as holding the life-giving power of the Earth itself.
>
> —Sharon Blackie, *If Women Rose Rooted*

Other examples of Gaia

Mother Teresa, Rachel Carson, David Attenborough, Mahatma Gandhi

Reflections on the Gaia in you

Do you recognize the Goddess Gaia in you?

Is the Earth Mother an archetype you strongly identify with?

How long has she been in you?

List the ways Gaia manifests in you.

What gifts does the Gaia in you bring?

Any shadows?

Who are some other women who embody the Goddess Gaia?

2

))))) ● (((((

Selene

Goddess of
the Moon

Archetype: Lunar Feminine

In order to reclaim our full selves, to integrate each of
these aspects through which we pass over the course of
our lives, we must first learn to embrace them though
our cycles.

—Lucy H. Pearce, *Moon Time*

Selene mythology

Selene was the Greek Goddess of the Moon. She and her siblings Helios, the Sun, and Eos, the Dawn, were born to the Titan deities Hyperion and Theia. Selene's Roman counterpart was the Goddess Luna.

Traditionally depicted as a beautiful young woman wearing a crown with a symbolic lunar sphere or crescent, Selene is also often shown riding a bull or a silvery chariot drawn by two winged horses. During the day she bathed in the waters of Oceanus, the river which encircled the world, and each night, after her brother Helios came home, she would traverse the sky, providing the night sky with its light.

Selene had many children with Gods and mortals, but her most enduring love was with a mortal man, the shepherd prince Endymion. Taken by the beauty of the shepherd, the moon Goddess longed to spend eternity with Endymion. She, though, was immortal, while he would age and die.

But Endymion was granted eternal youth and immortality by Zeus and placed in a state of eternal slumber in a cave near the peak of Mount Latmos. Thereafter, Selene visited him every night. Endymion slept with his eyes open, so that he too could gaze upon his lover. With Endymion, Selene gave birth to the Menai, the 50 Goddesses of the lunar months.

In Ancient Greece, the moon was important for the passage of time would be measured by it; the ancient Greek months being made up of three ten-day periods based on the phases of the moon. Magic and witchcraft are associated with the moon, particularly around the full moon, believing lunar energies manifest change or transformation.

A number of other Goddesses were also associated with the moon; however, only Selene was thought of as the moon incarnate.

Selene archetype: Lunar Feminine (Maiden, Mother, Wild Woman, Crone)

The Lunar Feminine is associated with the essence of human existence: love, romance, passion, fertility, mystery, magic, death, rebirth and the afterlife. This archetype has much to teach us about the eternal rhythms of the universe, the powers of nature, and the magical potential that is ours to tap into when we align our intentions with lunar energy.

Every woman goes through four archetypal phases of the Lunar Feminine: Maiden, Mother, Wild Woman and Crone. Each archetype corresponds to a different season, a different phase of the moon, and a different phase of the menstrual cycle. All are interconnected.

A woman's connection to the moon mirrors her own natural internal rhythms. Throughout a woman's life the feminine is ever changing, ushering in new phases and new chapters, each with their own unique magic.

Similarly, the moon goes through four distinct phases that are always changing and moving: new moon, waxing moon, full moon and waning moon. As the moon cycles, approximately every 29 days, a woman's body moves through the same cycle and rhythm throughout the month.

Each archetypal phase also corresponds to a season in a woman's life. And just as nature moves through different seasons in a year, women also move through an inner winter, inner spring, inner summer and inner autumn with every menstrual cycle.

It doesn't matter whether a woman has a regular cycle, is infertile, or no longer bleeds; she still cycles, because women are cyclic beings. This means the moon and the archetypes are always present within them. Tuning into your sacred cycle, therefore, along with the four Lunar Feminine archetypes, allows us to celebrate the Divine Feminine within, and without.

The four phases of a woman and the Lunar Feminine

Maiden

The Maiden is the first phase of womanhood. This coincides with a woman's first menstrual cycle. It is sometimes known as the first rite. This stage of life is filled with positivity, dreams and youthful ebullience.

————————

Season: spring

Moon phase: waxing moon

————————

The Maiden archetype is the energy type that women embody during the pre-ovulation, or the follicular phase of their own personal moon cycles (when bleeding has just finished).

This archetypal energy coincides with the waxing lunar phases — the waxing crescent, first quarter and waxing gibbous phases. The Maiden embodies innocence, receptivity and sexual inexperience.

Light: innocence, youthful, ebullient, receptive, creative, intuitive

Shadow: emotional co-dependency, diffidence, lack of autonomy, compliant, erratic, may be enticed into dangerous relationships

Mother

The next phase is the mother. A woman embodies this phase when she carries a life inside her. This phase is filled with strong nurturing energy, care, patience and protection.

Even if a woman does not physically carry children, she can still enter this phase. By bringing something new into the world that did not exist before, she becomes the mother of her own creations. It could be a garden, music, art, a book, a business, or adopting or fostering a child or a pet.

———————

Season: summer

Moon phase: full moon

———————

The Mother archetype breathes into life after the Maiden, at the full moon, rising within, during the ovulatory phase of a woman's cycle

   Light: nurturing, persistent, compassionate, generous, grounded

   Shadow: self-neglect, stubborn, possessive, over-controlling, over-protective, lack of boundaries

Wild Woman

The Wild Woman or Enchantress phase begins during a woman's menopause. It is a stage when the menstrual cycle stops and women can look inwards. It is a time when women can reclaim themselves and return to their instinctive nature, possibly after decades of caring for others.

The Wild Woman is a powerful transition for a woman. She owns her sexuality and is a force to be reckoned with. This Enchantress embodies the feminine mystique and trusts her intuition. Women in this phase often have a higher sex drive, where sex is for pleasure rather than procreation.

———————

Season: autumn

Moon phase: waning moon

———————

The Wild Woman emerges after the full moon, after ovulation. Many women dread this part of their cycle as it can be physically painful, emotional, and often brings out the darker, destructive sides of their psyches.

The Wild Woman is a healer, the untamed one, the awakening soul who will not rest. This archetype is *wild* because it is intrinsic to her nature.

> **Light:** passionate, adventurous, creative, intuitive, independent, brave, persuasive, fulfilled, confident, sensual, sexual, wild in every sense
>
> **Shadow:** loss of self when children move on, physical, mental or emotional pain, darkness, denial and destruction

Crone

Around the time of the waning crescent, and dark moon phases, when this energy moves through a woman's womb, the last of the four archetypes, the Crone, reveals herself. This final stage embodies wisdom, when women have aged and matured. This archetype has a more internal focus and is deeply connected to the Divine.

After years of nourishing and growing, Crones now evolve into wise women. This is a sacred phase filled with wisdom, teaching, compassion, transformation and healing laughter. The Crone archetype strengthens our belief and confidence in age-accumulated knowledge, insights and intuitions which enable women to stand up for their rights.

———————

Season: winter

Moon phase: new moon

———————

In contemporary western culture, the Crone archetype is probably the least valued. She has come to represent ageing and loss: loss of fertility, external beauty, activity and youth. But she has exchanged this for being valued as the keeper of stories, of experience, wisdom and knowledge, all of which she shares freely in order to guide others.

> **Light:** kind, compassionate and wise, mysterious, magical and prophetic, strong, fierce and protective, holds others to higher ethical standards
>
> **Shadow:** invisible, isolated, externally disconnected, lonely, lacks a sense of belonging and purpose

Selene in others

Selene manifests in every woman, each in her own unique way, at each particular stage in her life, and uniquely throughout every successive stage. To demonstrate this, I will use four different women to show how the Goddess of the Moon has manifested in each woman at a particular time in their lives — Emma Watson, Céline Dion, Melinda French Gates and Judi Dench.

Also, to demonstrate how a woman cycles through each successive phase of the Lunar Feminine archetypes, I will use Isabel Allende's personal reminisces from her book, *The Soul of a Woman*, to show how Selene manifested in Isabel throughout her life, how each archetype has been part of her personality for most of her life, and how at one particular phase, the shadow aspect of her personality was in the ascendancy.

Emma Watson (1990–) Maiden

Emma Watson is a British actress and activist. She was chosen for the lead role of Hermione Granger in the *Harry Potter and the Philosopher's Stone* film when she was nine. The character was brainy, bossy, nit-picking and a voice of reason.

Emma had just turned eleven when the first movie was released and between 2001 and 2011 she appeared in all eight Harry Potter films. The film series was one of the most successful in history and cemented Emma's role as a leading young female actor.

The Maiden archetype in Emma embodies creativity, intuition and the ability to transform herself. As a dominant Maiden, she learnt to embrace her natural strengths and to take control of her life; to shed passivity and self-consciousness, and to become confident and firmly rooted.

In 2005, she began a modelling career, appearing on the cover of *Teen Vogue* at the age of fifteen. The budding fashionista also acted as an adviser for People Tree, an ethical fashion label committed to promoting sustainable fashion.

Gifted academically, Emma achieved outstanding high school results despite long hours working on the films. As the Harry Potter franchise came to an end, she was keen to branch into new endeavours, but first a college education called. Emma studied in the United States at Brown University, then Worcester College, University of Oxford, graduating with a BA in English literature.

In 2014, Emma was appointed a UN Women Goodwill Ambassador, where she sought to refresh the concept of feminism and to include men in the process. In recent years, she has become a spokesperson on women's rights and other social issues, as well as continuing her film career.

Emma embodies the Maiden's innocence, independence and strength. With the rising energy of an emerging young woman, full of enthusiasm and authenticity, she is stunningly confident in her own skin.

> If you truly pour your heart in to what you believe in, even if it makes you vulnerable, amazing things can and will happen.
> —Emma Watson

Isabel Allende (1942–) Maiden

Writer Isabel Allende believes her feminism began at a very young age, when she saw her mother, abandoned with three young children, forced to become dependent on men. She became obsessed with justice and developed a visceral reaction to male chauvinism. Angry and often rebellious, Isabel was expelled from school at age six, accused of insubordination. 'It was a prelude to my future,' she has said.

Isabel never accepted the limited feminine role imposed on her by her family, society, culture and religion. As a teenager, while other girls may have been worried about their appearance and how to attract boys, she was preaching socialism and feminism, 'guided by an irresistible impulse' to define herself as a woman on her own terms and despite her mother's warnings that with her character she was never going to get married.

Isabel got her first job at seventeen, as a secretary. With her first pay cheque she bought pearl earrings for her mother, then started saving for marriage.

While she may not yet have the wisdom of age, the Maiden is fresh, new to experiences and her energy holds a gentle naivety which can veer between foolhardiness and contradiction. This shadow aspect of Isabel's personality was seen at various times in her life.

Isabel Allende as Mother

'Fearing spinsterhood, I somehow managed to trap a boyfriend. The romantic in me clung to him desperately.'

Isabel married at twenty and soon became a mother of two, saying of pregnancy and birth, 'that transcendent experience, which men still can't have, defined my existence'. While she loved her husband and remembers the first years with her young children as a very happy time, Isabel felt bored and stifled until she joined the staff of *Paula* magazine, where writing provided an outlet for her burning restlessness and where, she said, 'I was comfortable in my skin for the first time'.

The magazine challenged hundreds of taboos directly related to women, including abortion, infidelity, prostitution and motherhood and the demands, sacrifice and total denial of motherhood and the family.

Here, Isabel embodies the tension created in women where the mother archetype co-exists with the Wild Woman and other more independent and goal-oriented archetypes.

Céline Dion (1968–) Mother

Like many women who embody the Mother archetype, Canadian singer Céline Dion wanted a family with her husband and love of her life, René Angélil. She longed to become a mother so badly that she endured a painful, unsuccessful path to motherhood for years without giving up. No matter how much money she had, or how famous she became, Céline felt that only motherhood would lead her to a true sense of fulfilment and accomplishment. But realizing her dream of becoming a mother was not easy.

The couple tried unsuccessfully for six years before Céline took a break from singing to focus solely on starting a family. Fertility clinics, specialist consultations, treatments, surgical procedures and in-vitro fertilization (IVF) finally resulted in the birth of a son in 2001. Her perseverance had eventually paid off. She was now a mother. 'I think we are very blessed to have the opportunity and a blessing to be a mother,' she said. 'I think when you are, when you have a child, it's like there's another heart that grows inside of you. You have this like second heart.'

But for Céline and her husband, their family was not yet complete. To become pregnant again meant Céline had to go through yet another roller-coaster ride. She underwent more IVF cycles, suffered a miscarriage, endured repeated rounds of hormone shots, blood tests and injections to increase her chances of becoming pregnant, but nothing worked. The disappointing results kept coming.

It was a highly emotional struggle for Céline and Angélil, but they were determined to keep trying. Nearly ten years after her first child, Céline gave birth to twin boys in 2010.

> I've worked hard for nearly 30 years and I feel like only now is it paying off in terms of happiness ...
> There's nothing that can top being a mother.
> —Céline Dion

Melinda French Gates (1964–) Wild Woman

American philanthropist, one of the world's most powerful and wealthy women, and mother of three, Melinda French Gates is the former wife of Microsoft founder Bill Gates, and co-chair of the Bill and Melinda Gates Foundation. For the past two decades, this formidable pair has strived to improve education, global health and other causes through their namesake foundation.

In 2019, Melinda released her book, *The Moment of Lift: How empowering women changes the world*. It was a call to action for women's empowerment. The book tells of Melinda's journey from a partner working behind the scenes to one of the world's foremost advocates for women, driven by the belief that no one should be excluded, all lives have equal value, and gender equity is the crucial lever that lifts everything.

In 2021, Melinda and Bill Gates announced that, after a great deal of thought and a lot of work on their relationship, they were ending their 27-year marriage, stating that although they planned to continue as co-chairs and trustees of their foundation, 'we no longer believe we can grow together as a couple in the next phase of our lives'. And in her own personal moment of uplift, the petition for divorce filed by Melinda Gates cited that, 'this marriage is irretrievably broken'.

For Melinda, as for most women, the Wild Woman phase was a powerful transition. After decades of caring for others it was time for her to finally reclaim her own personal freedom, the freedom to choose her own destiny. Like many women, divorces, drastic lifestyle changes and bold steps are taken as an instinctive nature calls them to return to their true selves and recall who they are: their deep quintessential selves. In her own words:

> All women everywhere, have the same hopes:
> we want to be self-sufficient and create better
> lives for ourselves and our loved ones.
> —Melinda French Gates

Isabel Allende as Wild Woman

After the political coup in Chile, Isabel and her family fled to Argentina but living in exile undermined the marriage. With her career, Isabel had had a place to funnel her passion, but now she didn't and her shadow side was demanding attention. 'The stability of our marriage had felt stifling before, but I'd managed to bat the feelings away … Nobody can suppress themselves forever.'

An Argentinian musician wandered into the perfect storm that was her life. Isabel fell madly in love and ran away to Spain with her lover, leaving her children behind. She didn't even say goodbye to them. The Mother in her was much less dominant than the Wild Woman, but she had crossed boundaries. She knew it; her children knew it, and felt it. Isabel returned two months later, but it took a decade to heal her relationship with her children. 'I confess, though, that sometimes my passionate heart clouds my understanding … I couldn't put out this new fire. I was consumed by it.'

This same fiery passion was very much in evidence in her writing, but in a form more readily embraced. Isabel went on to write 26 best-selling books. Over the course of her life and three marriages, the third when she was 77, Isabel has grown as a woman and revels in the rewards of embracing one's sexuality. 'Passion, I know now, can destroy you as much as define you.'

The Wild Woman in Isabel is the original rebel. She represents that unshaken and integral part of all women that is a sacred true being.

Isabel Allende as Crone

Now in her seventies, with the Crone archetype in ascendancy, Isabel's wisdom shines through. She realizes that her plan to remain active may fail, but hopes that the last things to go will be her writing and sensuality. 'While my body deteriorates, my soul rejuvenates.'

Isabel is now more distracted, but less angry; her character has softened a little, but her passion for the causes she embraced and the people she loves has increased. She does not fear her vulnerability because she no longer confuses it with weakness. Since her daughter's untimely death, and although aware of death's proximity, Isabel now considers it a friend. 'In brief, I am in a splendid moment of my destiny ... This is the stage of kindness.'

Isabel set up the Isabel Allende Foundation in 1996 in homage to her late daughter Paula. It invests in securing women and girls reproductive rights, economic independence, and freedom from violence. A tribute to the Goddesses Selene and Gaia in her.

Judi Dench (1934–) Crone

Iconic British actress Judi Dench has developed a reputation as one of the greatest actresses of the post-war period. The Oscar-winning matriarch, heralded as one of Britain's beloved national treasures, is also a Goddess of the Moon and in the Crone phase of her life. But her dogged determination and *joie de vivre* will ensure she does 'not go gentle into that good night'.

The Crone archetype may bring physical limitations. Judi's failing eyesight has forced her to give up driving, which she says was one of the most traumatic moments of her life. Now she employs someone to read her scripts to her, but, 'I am tired of being told I'm too old to try something ... age is a number, something imposed on you ... It drives me absolutely spare when people ask, "When are you going to retire?"'

As with Judi, who is a healthy inner Crone, an older woman finds her ability to unflinchingly speak truth to power. She is both fierce and compassionate. Judi now sports a tattoo on her wrist, given to her by her daughter, a present for her 81st birthday, which says fittingly, *carpe diem*, or seize the day.

A widow for nine years, Judi is now in a relationship with conservationist, David Mills. When speaking about her love life in an interview with *Hello!* magazine, she said, 'Well of course, you still feel desire. The need for intimacy doesn't ever go away.'

The Crone is a spiritual archetype, in tune with the sacredness of nature. Nowhere is this more exemplified than in Judi's deep love of trees. The documentary *My Passion for Trees* was a magical study of the changing seasons and their effect on the lives of the trees in Judi's own secret woodland close to her home.

The Crone is the guide between the realms — embracing dark and light. This archetype heralds an important transition, the onset of metaphorical death, and with it, renewal.

Other examples of Selene

Katy Perry, Catherine, Duchess of Cambridge, Mackenzie Scott, Dame Maggie Smith

Reflections on the Selene in you

Do you recognize the Goddess Selene in you?

Is the Lunar Feminine an archetype you strongly identify with?

In what ways does the Lunar Feminine manifest in you?

What phase of life are you in?

Which phase resonates most with you at this time in your life?

In what ways are you in tune with the rhythms of nature?

What gifts does the Selene in you bring?

Any shadows?

Who are some other women who embody the Goddess Selene?

3

Eos

Goddess of the Dawn

Archetype: Solar Feminine

The Goddess does not rule the world. She is the world.
Manifest in each of us. She can be known internally by
every individual, in all her magnificent diversity.

—Starhawk, *The Spiral Dance: A rebirth of the ancient
religions of the great goddess*

Eos mythology

Eos is the Greek Goddess of the Dawn. She is a Titan, the daughter of Hyperion and Theia, and the sister of Helios, God of the Sun, and Selene, Goddess of the Moon. Her Roman counterpart is Aurora. As an elemental Goddess embodying the power of nature, Eos has divine authority and absolute control over light.

Eos was the most resplendent of all the beings in the Greek pantheon. With the brilliant dye of saffron as her chosen colour, she is associated with roses, which embody the glowing hues of the dawn. Depicted as a beautiful rosy maiden with large wings, she bears a star on her forehead and a torch in her hand.

With her purple cape wrapped around her, Eos rose into the sky at the start of each day. In her glorious golden chariot drawn by winged horses, she opened the gates of heaven. Her rays of light dispersed the mists of night; to announce to all the gods and mortals the coming of sunlight. As she passed, the tender plants and flowers, revived by the morning dew, lifted their heads to welcome her.

Not only did Eos announce the arrival of her brother Helios, the God of the Sun, but she also accompanied him during the day until he had finished traversing the sky in his own golden chariot. At night she would rest in her home near the river Oceanus to be ready for the next day.

The Goddess of the Dawn had many divine lovers and is credited with being the mother of the four winds and the five planets, or wandering stars. Once, after Eos had bedded Aphrodite's lover, Ares, Aphrodite put a spell on her. Because of it, Eos had an unquenchable desire for handsome young men. Her favourite consort was Tithonos, Prince of Troy, with whom she had some notable offspring — King Memnon of Ethiopia and his brother Emathion, King of Arabia, heroes of the Trojan War.

Eos personified the glory of the new day and symbolized hope, rejuvenation and rebirth.

Eos archetype: Solar Feminine (Visionary, Leader, Doyenne, Creative)

The Solar Feminine is not one archetype. It can be found in vision, power, achievement and artistic expression.

With their power and creativity, the great fire Goddesses of ancient civilizations were the embodiment of Solar Feminine energy. But with the rise of patriarchal societies, roles were manipulated to exclude Solar Feminine archetypes; the fact that women could be powerful creators was overlooked.

Women's creative functions were limited to childbirth, and the lunar Goddesses became the mothers and keepers of feminine energy on Earth. Humans were conditioned to define masculine and feminine as oppositional, and to assign solar energy to the male and lunar energy to the female. But the ancients knew better, worshipping both solar Goddesses and lunar Gods.

Somewhat belatedly, the world is once again recognizing Solar Feminine energy and Lunar Masculine energy. The Solar Feminine embodies yang energy, strength, passion, creativity and action; qualities that have not been appreciated in females since the matrilineal era some 6000 years ago.

The Solar Feminine is different from the Lunar Feminine, whose yin energy is gentle, receptive, intuitive and nurturing. Women have been conditioned to identify more with the Lunar Feminine energy. To be a woman and to embody solar energy has been more difficult because power, authority and wealth most often reside with men. Those women who have attempted to express their solar energy have often modelled the Solar Masculine, which can wreak havoc with their inner lives and relationships. To become whole, a woman must learn to integrate the gentle, nurturing and receptive qualities of her Lunar Feminine with the intense, driven qualities of her Solar Feminine. To be caring and strong at the same time.

With increased acceptance of the Solar Feminine energy, the archetypal model of the Fire Goddess and her fierce, fiery yet feminine power and creativity, women feel more comfortable with who and what they are, and what they can achieve. The Solar Feminine is a creative energy, but that creativity is channelled in entrepreneurial ways, in many diverse professions, to achieve status and success in different ways.

Being able to move an understanding of the masculine and feminine energies beyond dualism and into complexity helps break the patterns of dualistic thinking and the judgments that so often go with them. Women, and men, will no longer be trapped in either/or scenarios, but can choose whatever aspects appeal to them at that time in their lives. To better align their lives in a way that most suits their sense of who they are.

The Solar Feminine is a strong, dynamic, creative, passionate and radiant feminine energy, fuelled by passion and purpose and cushioned by compassion, that creates a powerful impetus for positive change. For a woman to fully embrace her Solar Feminine nature takes great courage, but it will be the enabler for new freedoms and creativity; for women to reclaim their power.

> **Light:** strong, passionate, energetic, creative, powerful, forward-thinking, action-oriented, inspiring, courageous, compassionate
>
> **Shadow:** lack of balance, driven, pushing too hard, using power to exploit others, so focused on the big picture can forget the importance of relationships, fragmentation

Eos in others

As with the other elemental Goddesses, Gaia and Selene, the potential for Eos can be found in every woman, but cultural and social norms often mean that a woman's ability to bring light to the world is undervalued, and is therefore a less well-developed or hidden aspect of a woman's personality. Breaking down barriers is crucial to finding the Eos within.

The examples of Eos I am using exemplify vision, power, achievement and artistic expression, and the use of those attributes to ignite the fire of goodness, the Goddess within. In lighting the way, Marie Curie, Christine Lagarde, Oprah Winfrey and Madonna all overcame significant obstacles to realize their magnificent, multifarious dreams; to showcase a world of possibility and passion for others to emulate.

In contrast, Ghislaine Maxwell inherited fame and fortune and then used her power, wealth and privilege to traduce cultural and social norms and consequently become a social pariah.

Marie Curie (1867–1934)

Polish–French physicist Marie Curie became the first woman to win a Nobel Prize and the first person — man or woman — to win the award twice. Marie's efforts, with her husband Pierre Curie, led to the discovery of polonium and radium and, after Pierre's death, the further development of X-rays.

As a child, Marie had a bright and curious mind and excelled at school. But despite being a top student in her secondary school, she could not attend the male-only University of Warsaw. Instead, she studied at Warsaw's floating university, a set of secret, underground, informal classes.

Marie dreamed of going abroad to earn an official degree but lacked the financial resources to pay for more studies. Undeterred, for five years she worked as a tutor and a governess, using her spare time to study physics, chemistry and mathematics.

In 1891, Marie enrolled at the Sorbonne in Paris. By 1894 she had earned a master's degree in physics, another degree in mathematics and had met French physicist Pierre Curie. They married in 1895. At first, they worked on separate projects, but after Marie discovered radioactivity Pierre put aside his own work to help with her research. In time, the devoted couple welcomed two daughters — Irène in 1897 and Ève in 1904.

Despite her grief when Pierre was killed in 1906, Marie took over her husband's job at the Sorbonne, becoming the institution's first female professor. Marie continued her research while raising her daughters and overseeing their education; she was a beacon of light and hope.

Her oldest daughter became a scientist, working alongside her mother and winning her own Nobel Prize. Marie's younger daughter became a journalist and author who won the National Book Award for a biography of her mother.

> I am one of those who think like Nobel, that humanity will draw more good than evil from new discoveries.
> —Marie Curie

Christine Lagarde (1956–)

The creative energy of the Solar Feminine can be harnessed to achieve status and success in differing ways, as exemplified by Christine Lagarde, French politician, economist and lawyer. In May 1968, when she was a teenager, French schools were shut down during a student uprising. As her fellow pupils took to the streets, Lagarde took up synchronized swimming. It helped her both personally and in her subsequent political career: 'It was synchronized swimming that taught me to grit your teeth and smile. In exactly the same way, it's a sport of resistance and endurance. You're in tension and control.'

In 2019 the combination of her innate intelligence, strict work and study ethic, and her unique ability to negotiate the male-dominated world in which she operated without sacrificing her femininity led to Christine becoming the first woman president of the European Central Bank. It was the latest high in a career that saw her become the first woman to head the International Monetary Fund (IMF), the first female finance minister of a G8 economy, and the first woman chair of an international law firm. Her rise was extraordinary, as was the depth and breadth of her power. She is now number two on the *Forbes* list of the world's most powerful women. But to Christine, 'success is never complete. It's an endless combat. Each morning one must put one's capacities to the test once again.'

Although she works in mostly competitive male environments, Christine realizes the importance of paving the way for other women to follow in her Solar Feminine footsteps.

> Don't try to imitate the boys. Be yourselves
> and support each other.
> —Christine Lagarde

Oprah Winfrey (1954–)

Influential American talk show host, television producer, actress, author and philanthropist, Oprah Winfrey is a shining light, a fire Goddess in her own right.

Oprah had a difficult childhood and lived in great poverty, and was given up by her unmarried parents soon after her birth. Her first six years were spent with her grandmother and then her mother. She was repeatedly sexually abused during her youth.

When Oprah's behaviour became problematic, she was sent to live with her father. It was a turning point. A strict disciplinarian who demanded a great deal from her, he helped to inspire her self-confidence and self-discipline. She became an honours student at Tennessee State University, where she joined the university drama club, the debating club and the student council. After graduating, Oprah started in broadcasting.

Her talk shows and books were ground-breaking. Focusing on many issues facing American women, and black women in particular, Oprah became a powerful role model and advocate. She was instrumental in highlighting discrimination and prejudice, and breaking down barriers, showing how to 'turn your wounds into wisdom'. Oprah has helped shape cultural trends and promoted various humanitarian and philanthropic causes.

A shrewd entrepreneur, Oprah has used her success in television as a springboard into other ventures, such as films and her own production company. She is now one of the richest self-made women in the world, which allows her to pursue other goals and initiatives that really matter to her, like making a difference in other people's lives. Just as she has with her own.

> What I learned at a very early age was that I was responsible for my life … you create your own reality by the way you think and therefore act. You cannot blame apartheid, your parents, your circumstances, because you are not your circumstances. You are your possibilities.
>
> —Oprah Winfrey

Madonna (1958–)

Born Madonna Louise Ciccone, Madonna is an American singer, actress, dancer and entrepreneur. Although raised as a Roman Catholic, after losing her mother at an early age she rebelled against her traditional upbringing by turning her conservative clothing into revealing outfits, frequenting nightclubs and turning her back on her religious background.

But Madonna balanced the insubordinate side of her personality with a drive for perfectionism and high achievement. She was a straight-A student, cheerleader and disciplined dancer, her hard work earning her a full scholarship to the University of Michigan dance program, but she dropped out and moved to New York. 'I had a dream,' she said. 'I wanted to be a big star. I didn't know anybody. I wanted to dance. I wanted to sing. I wanted to do all those things. I wanted to make people happy. I wanted to be famous. I worked really hard and my dream came true.'

Madonna is now the best-selling female artist of all time and has sold over 300 million records worldwide. Known as the queen of pop (a title given by the media), Madonna has shaped music culture. This visionary artist pursued an independent and experimental approach to her career — writing most of her own songs and constantly redefining her image, often in collaboration with top designers, photographers and directors. Madonna was the first female artist to realize the power of the music video.

Pushing the boundaries of taste and behaviour, Madonna often courted controversy by upsetting religious and moral sensibilities with her distinctive sexual and satirical images. In spite of this, her immense popularity allowed her to achieve levels of power and control that were unprecedented for a woman in the entertainment industry.

But that came at a cost. In her acceptance speech for *Billboard*'s Woman of the Year in 2016, Madonna thanked them for acknowledging her ability to continue her 34-year career in the face of blatant sexism, misogyny, constant bullying and relentless abuse, and the way she coped. For her, 'in life there is no real safety except self-belief'.

Most of Madonna's relationships have been lived in the spotlight, with the same controversial style very much in evidence in her personal life. Her marriage to Sean Penn was tumultuous. Eventually, they divorced, but remain close. Madonna had a daughter with boyfriend Carlos Leon, before marrying Guy Ritchie. She and Ritchie had one child together, a son, before divorcing. Since then, Madonna has dated a series of men. While she has received some criticism for her habit of dating younger men, she is not seemingly bothered by the negativity. She describes herself thus, 'I'm anal retentive. I'm a workaholic. I have insomnia. And I'm a control freak. That's why I'm not married. Who could stand me?'

Madonna created more controversy as she negotiated the complexities of the Malawi court system to adopt four Malawian children and successfully blend an unconventional family of six children. Madonna embodies Eos, the fierce and fiery Goddess who did it her way.

> I am my own experiment. I am my own work of art.
> —Madonna

Ghislaine Maxwell (1961–)

British socialite Ghislaine Maxwell, daughter of disgraced British media tycoon Robert Maxwell, was born into fame and fortune. She was vivacious, gifted, Oxford-educated, spoke several languages and was very close to her father. Like many Solar Feminine archetypes, Ghislaine sought status and success in her own right. She personified vision, power and ambition, but her goals seemed more targeted towards personal or familial aggrandisement.

Robert Maxwell's money provided Ghislaine with status and connections to business and society elite. She was initially sent to New York to pave her father's way when he bought the *Daily News*. After his death, she made the United States her home.

Ghislaine soon became part of the inner circle of Jeffrey Epstein, wealthy financier and convicted sex offender; she remained there for more than a decade. Reportedly, they were briefly lovers; she remained his closest friend and confidante, with Ghislaine introducing Epstein to many of her wealthy and powerful friends. She facilitated his social contacts, flying with him on his private jet and organizing dinners for influential people at his homes.

It was a world of unimaginable decadence. The epicentres were Epstein's opulent New York Upper East Side townhouse and his Palm Beach mansion. The rarefied circles which were Epstein's and Ghislaine's milieu included Nobel laureates, presidents, heads of states, British royals, Wall Street power brokers and A-listers in every glamorous profession. They remained secure in the embrace of fame and fortune, until Epstein was arrested in 2019 on federal sex-trafficking and conspiracy charges connected to the sexual abuse of underage girls.

When he was found dead of an apparent suicide in prison soon after, Ghislaine came into the public eye. Epstein's alleged victims have accused her of being deeply involved in his criminal activities. At her trial, several women testified that she was Epstein's primary co-conspirator and madam whose job it was to recruit young women into his orbit. At the time of writing, convicted on five criminal charges related to the trafficking and sexual abuse of young women and girls, Ghislaine awaits sentencing.

Like other Solar Feminine archetypes, Ghislaine broke through barriers; she pushed the boundaries of taste and behaviour to extremes. But, as happens when the shadow aspects of a personality dominate, with Ghislaine and Epstein there were disparate interpretations about what constitutes social or antisocial behaviour, to whom the laws apply, and whose interests those laws are designed to protect.

Ghislaine once enjoyed a highly regarded, extravagant and luxurious lifestyle, which attracted many of the rich and famous into her orbit, but it has lost its lustre. She is now a pariah, who will languish in prison for many years to come. In the court of public opinion, Ghislaine was condemned for ruthlessly using her power, privilege and sense of entitlement to exploit others.

Other examples of Eos

Agatha Christie, Estée Lauder, Julia Gillard, Kim Kardashian

Reflections on the Eos in you

Do you recognize the Goddess Eos in you?

Is the Solar Feminine an archetype you strongly identify with?

How long has Eos been in you?

List the ways Eos manifests in you.

What gifts does the Eos in you bring?

Any shadows?

Who are some other women who embody the Goddess Eos?

4

Artemis

Goddess of the Hunt and the Moon

Archetype: Huntress

Within every woman there is a wild and natural creature,
a powerful force, filled with good instincts, passionate
creativity and ageless knowing. Her name is Wild Woman,
but she is an endangered species.

—Clarissa Pinkola Estés, *Women Who Run with the Wolves*

Artemis mythology

Artemis, the Greek Goddess of the Hunt, the Moon, Chastity and Childbirth, is an independent Goddess, or virgin Goddess as they were known in ancient Greece. Virgin didn't mean chaste. It meant self-reliant; they exist in their own right.

Artemis, known to the Romans as Diana, is the tall, lovely daughter of Leto and Zeus. She is the firstborn twin sister of Apollo and assisted her mother during an extremely difficult and painful labour of her brother. At three years old, she first met her father, Zeus, who was so pleased with her courage and beauty that he offered her anything she wished.

Artemis chose a bow and arrow, a pack of hounds to hunt with, mountains and wilderness to live in, nymphs to follow her, a chiton (tunic) to run in, and to be allowed to stay a virgin forever. Zeus granted all her wishes, plus the privilege of making the selections herself.

The older Artemis is a beautiful, slender young woman with golden curls, much taller than all her companions. The Goddess of the Hunt has a spiritual bond with nature, roaming the fields, forests, mountains and nearby springs with her nymphs and hunting dogs. Or riding in a chariot pulled by four golden deer. In pursuit of her prey, her aim is unerring. But, as a Goddess of Wildlife, she also protects it, especially young animals.

As Goddess of the Moon, Artemis is a light bearer, carrying torches in her hands, or with the moon and stars around her head. She is often seen dancing and revelling in moonlight celebrations and rituals, accompanied by her nymphs and sacred animals.

Artemis' virginity is seen as symbolic of her authority, power and independence, and signifies that she is in charge of her own life and destiny.

64

As such, this gives her equality with the Gods of the pantheon. Artemis also defended the innocence of her worshippers and was merciless if any one of her priestesses lost her purity. Her wrath was legendary.

The Goddess of the Hunt and the Moon is a proud, wild, instinctive and competitive spirit, with a deep affinity for the wilderness and wild animals and a profound bond with her band of nymphs. A passionate protectress of the young, the powerless and women experiencing childbirth, Artemis is one of the most beloved Goddesses, honoured in art, songs and rituals.

Artemis archetype: Huntress (Competitor, Sister, Protector)

As Goddess of the Hunt and the Moon, Artemis is the personification of the wild, free, feminine spirit. This complex and multifaceted Goddess is likely to be a lifelong part of a woman's psyche.

The back-to-nature Artemis and her association with the wilderness and hunting has led her to become the archetypal seeker, embarking on a journey of discovery, or exploring new fields, often preferring her own company over that of society.

Like Artemis, the Huntress archetype tends towards perfectionism and fears conformity, thus becoming known for seeking individuality and freedom in both her inner and outer worlds. This archetype governs a woman's relationship with power, how she wields her will and determines her ability to take action in the world. Her gifts include autonomy, freedom, choice, physical and mental strength, power and perseverance.

The Huntress archetype personifies a woman's innermost desire to act independently, achieve great things and focus on the goals she's most passionate about. She is the embodiment of female dominance, success, freedom and fearlessness.

When we embody our Huntress energy, we stand up for what we believe in, ask for what we want, set a healthy boundaries and balance our needs with those of others. We are confident, assertive, trust our own judgment and have a healthy sense of self-esteem and self-worth.

The Artemis archetype is a natural competitor and is usually good at sports. In pursuit of her chosen goal, she will push herself to the limit. The Competitor archetype imbues a woman with courage, persistence and the innate ability to concentrate intensely on whatever she needs to succeed.

By nature, Artemis women have a strong sense of sisterhood and appreciate the company of other women. As the Sister archetype, Artemis represents qualities idealized by the feminist movement. Empowering qualities such as courage, concentration and initiative often make her the leader of important organizations and interest groups. Even Artemis women who are individualists have feminist leanings, as they see themselves as the equal of men.

Artemis, as the Protector archetype, stands up and speaks out without fear of rejection. Her strong sense for justice calls her into action for the protection and rescue of those who need her help. Young girls, women and animals in dire circumstances are all under her protection.

An Artemis woman needs to take care of her inner freedom and independence, especially when in closer relationships with men or women. Although not usually the motherly type, if she chooses to become a parent she will be very protective of her children, much like a mother bear. But she will raise children to be independent from an early age, just as she was.

Being a virgin Goddess, Artemis may lack the capacity for intimacy. To her, involvement in career, a creative project or cause will come before intimate relationships, which can make her appear emotionally detached from others and lacking a sense of empathy.

Artemis exemplifies the independent, achievement-oriented feminine spirit, the indomitable spirit of woman with the passion and perseverance not only to survive, but to thrive.

> **Light:** independence, skill, discipline, courage, goal-oriented, physical and mental strength, willpower, achievement, ambition, active
>
> **Shadow:** vengeful, impulsive, aloof, indifferent to suffering of others, victory at any cost, perfectionist, self-centred

Artemis in others

Artemis is a complex and multifaceted Goddess who embodies a range of archetypes. The examples I have chosen reflect this. There is the back-to-nature archetype, exemplified by Miriam Lancewood and Junko Tabei, the latter for whom mountain climbing was as much a spiritual as a physical feat. Then two elite athletes — Serena Williams and Marion Jones — contrasting the light and shadow aspects of the Huntress and the Competitor archetypes. And finally, the light and shadow aspects of Germaine Greer, the epitome of the independent, indomitable spirit of woman; the Sister archetype, who represents qualities idealized by the feminist movement.

Miriam Lancewood (1983–)

Best-selling Dutch author of *Woman in the Wilderness: A story of survival, love & self-discovery in New Zealand* and *Wild at Heart*, Miriam Lancewood has lived a nomadic life with her husband Peter, 30 years her senior, for a decade, including seven years in the remote New Zealand wilderness, first camping around the South Island and then walking the length of the country, over Te Araroa Trail.

The couple survived in extreme conditions by hunting wild animals and foraging edible plants, relying only on minimal supplies. They slept in a tent, or when the weather was atrocious took shelter in huts. Miriam described her life thus: 'My life is free, random and spontaneous. This in itself creates enormous energy and clarity in body and mind.'

Survival — finding food, shelter, firewood, building fires and preparing meals — was the focus of their days. A life-long vegetarian, Miriam transformed into the Huntress, using a bow and arrow to shoot possums, goats and hares, the meat providing vital nutrition, warmth and energy.

Miriam has spent most of her adult life living outdoors in the uninhabited wilderness. Like Artemis, she has come to know the wild intimately, is very much attuned to it, and has now mastered the art of surviving in it. 'Now I feel I can look after myself. Although I'm dependent on my rifle, I can survive by myself in the mountains by myself, and that's amazing. I'm happy about that. It gives me so much confidence.'

In 2020, because of Peter's renal failure, they lived in a house for the first time in a decade, but they plan to resume their nomadic lifestyle again soon.

Junko Tabei (1939–2016)

Japanese mountaineer Junko Tabei was the first woman to summit Mount Everest, and the first to climb the Seven Summits (the highest mountains on each continent). These feats called for more than just remarkable skill and fitness. Junko faced virulent mid-twentieth century sexism, defying cultural expectations for women, who, at the time and especially in Japan, were thought to be nothing more than homemakers.

Junko fell in love with climbing at ten years old and began climbing in earnest with a mountain climbing club while studying at university. Often, she was the only woman climbing or at meetings. Some men refused to climb with her but she persevered, and eventually formed her own club — this one for women climbers.

Junko said, 'Everest for me, and I believe for the world, is the physical and symbolic manifestation of overcoming odds to achieve a dream'. So, in 1975, the Japanese Women's Everest Expedition began working their way up the mountain. At 2700 metres (9000 ft), while camped beneath the Lhotse Face near Everest, an avalanche struck. Junko was buried and knocked unconscious. Miraculously, she was pulled from the debris by her team's Sherpas.

Unable to walk for the next two days, yet determined to finish what she had come to Nepal to do, Junko nevertheless summitted Mount Everest twelve days after the avalanche. She was the only woman in her party to do so, making it to the top on her hands and knees. By 1992, Junko had completed the Seven Summits. Her gritty determination and unwavering focus on her goals exemplifies the indomitable spirit of woman, and of the Artemis within.

As Artemis the Protectress, Junko returned to school in 2002 to study ecology. She became an influential figure in the fight to protect and preserve wild places, with particular focus on the environmental degradation of the Everest region. Junko didn't stop climbing until she was well into her seventies.

> Technique and ability alone do not get you to the top; it is the willpower that is most important. This willpower you cannot buy with money or be given by others … it rises from your heart.
>
> —Junko Tabei

Serena Williams (1981–)

American tennis player Serena Williams is the embodiment of Artemis the Huntress and the Competitor. When this archetype is dominant, a woman's primary concern is autonomy and achieving her personal goals, and she possesses an innate ability to be undistracted by competition or the needs of others.

Sometimes hailed as the greatest female tennis player of all time, Serena embodies what it means to be a strong and empowered woman. She and her sister Venus have dominated international tennis for over fifteen years, despite having to deal with a series of media controversies, serious injuries, racism and sexism. Serena revolutionized women's tennis with her powerful style of play and won 23 Grand Slam singles titles, more than any other woman or man during the open era. She believes, 'I've grown most not from victories, but setbacks. If winning is God's reward, then losing is how he teaches us.'

Serena learnt tennis from her father on the public courts in Los Angeles and turned professional in 1995, one year after her sister Venus. Many thought Venus would be the first to win a Grand Slam singles title, but it was the younger sister, Serena, who did, winning the 1999 US Open.

Serena is the ultimate archer. She takes up her racket and ball, and takes aim. But even for this Huntress, when she became a mother, and other archetypes came to the fore, life was harder to control.

> As an athlete, you can't be vulnerable. You have to be strong. As a mom, you're completely vulnerable to everything. And that's what makes it scary.
> —Serena Williams

Marion Jones (1975–)

Marion Jones is a Belizean–American former Olympian track and field athlete. This Huntress, the ultimate competitor, won three gold medals and two bronze medals at the 2000 Olympic Games in Sydney. Eight years later, she had been stripped of her medals and was in prison.

Marion drove herself. 'I train harder than anyone else in the world. Last year I was supposed to take a month off and I took three days off because I was afraid somebody out there was training harder. That's the feeling I go through … Am I not doing what someone else is doing? Is someone out there training harder than I am?'

When the light aspect of this archetype is dominant, a woman's primary concern is autonomy, achieving her own personal goals, and she has an innate ability to be undistracted by competition or the needs of others. Marion's shadow was focused on what others were doing, afraid that someone might be doing more than her, rather than concentrating on her own needs and goals.

Marion, a highly rated high school athlete, received a scholarship to attend the University of North Carolina to play basketball and run track. While there, she started dating C.J. Hunter, a shot putter and one of the track coaches. They married in 1998 and trained together in preparation for the 2000 Olympics in Sydney.

When Hunter tested positive for a banned steroid in Sydney pre-Olympic drug tests, Olympics officials took away his credentials and banned him from serving as his wife's coach. Inevitably, questions arose about whether Marion was clean. Despite the huge cloud hanging over her head, she performed well in her five Olympic events.

In 2002, Marion and Hunter divorced. She participated in the 2004 Athens Olympics but failed to win any medals. Later that year, Victor Conte, founder of Bay Area Laboratory Co-operative (BALCO) and steroids mastermind, publicly confessed that he had personally given Marion four different illegal performance-enhancing drugs before, during and after the 2000 Sydney Games. She denied the allegations.

Marion continued competing, but in October 2007, because of mounting pressure, she admitted to lying to federal agents under oath about her steroid use before the 2000 Olympics and also admitted to a cheque-cashing scheme. She pleaded guilty to both charges, announced her retirement and was later sentenced to six months in prison at Fort Worth, where she remained until her release in September 2008.

Victory at any cost had cost Marion dearly — personally and professionally.

Germaine Greer (1939–)

Australian writer and intellectual Germaine Greer was one of the major voices of the radical feminist movement in the latter half of the twentieth century. Her book, *The Female Eunuch*, changed lives. It inspired women to challenge the ties binding them to gender inequality and domestic servitude.

Germaine urged women to challenge the stereotypes patriarchal society had created for them, which limited their capacity to act. She compared women's lives to those of birds in captivity and told them, in a hopeful way, that life could be otherwise.

This passionate Huntress preached independence from men and male opinions by insisting sexual shibboleths should be smashed. Germaine famously drew attention to deeply entrenched cultural constructs that linked sex to shame and disgust, calling out the hypocrisy of a society that blamed women for men's misogyny. Her wrath, like Artemis's, was legendary.

Germaine declared women must question everything they had been taught about sex, love, romance, their bodies and their rights. Freedom was theirs, but they had to claim it; they had to take action. Germaine as sister, protector of other women, particularly those who have been oppressed. She believes, 'Freedom is fragile and must be protected. To sacrifice it, even as a temporary measure, is to betray it.'

In 2001, the Artemis within this controversial, confrontational and contrary character morphed again. Germaine fell in love and, unlike her earlier marriage, when she walked out after three weeks, this time she committed for life. 'The forest had me till death us do part.' She purchased Cave Creek, 60 hectares of Gondwana rainforest in south-east Queensland in Australia, with the intention of gradually rehabilitating the land, long degraded by agricultural clearances, and restoring the biodiversity of the original rainforest. Her book, *White Beech: The rainforest years*, documents her inspirational restoration of the rainforest in the hope that, 'it will convey the deep joy that rebuilding wild nature can bring. For me, it did. Let's hope that joy is also infectious.' And to encourage others to do the same, Germaine donated the land to Friends of the Gondwana Rainforest, a charity dedicated to the conservation of rainforests.

But Germaine is a multifaceted Artemis, whose shadow side is more in evidence as she ages. The outspokenness of this professional provocateur, the rallying cry for feminists in the 1970s to free them from the chains of oppression, is now more often perceived in a critical light, even by feminists and especially the #MeToo movement. Instead of advocating for a free and equal society, Germaine is now being accused of being culturally insensitive, apparently indifferent to the suffering of others, even misogynistic. In short, blaming the victim. Her recent public comments, like 'rape is just bad sex' and 'transgender women are not women', have caused a furore, as happened in the 1970s, but her insights now seem far less relevant to today's world — they could perhaps be likened to those of a self-centred and vengeful saboteur.

> If you spread your legs because he [Harvey Weinstein] said "be nice to me and I'll give you a job in a movie" then I'm afraid that's tantamount to consent, and it's too late now to start whingeing about that.

Germaine unleashes her words like an arrow. They are calculated, designed to be deliberately offensive, to hit the target, and to wound, if not kill. Leaving the Huntress in control to further her own ambition.

Other Examples of Artemis

Elizabeth I, Amelia Earheart, Gloria Steinem, Robyn Davidson

Reflections on the Artemis in you

Do you recognize the Goddess Artemis in you?

Is the Huntress an archetype you strongly identify with?

How long has Artemis been in you?

List the ways Artemis manifests in you.

What gifts does the Artemis in you bring?

Any shadows?

Who are some other women who embody the Goddess Artemis?

5

Athena

Goddess of Wisdom, War and Crafts

Archetype: Sage

A wise woman wishes to be no one's enemy; a wise
woman refuses to be anyone's victim.

—Maya Angelou

Athena mythology

Known to the Romans as Minerva, Athena is the Greek Goddess of Wisdom, War and Crafts and the adored patroness and protectress of the city of Athens. She is essentially urban and civilized, the opposite in many respects of Artemis, Goddess of the outdoors. But like Artemis, Athena is an independent Goddess dedicated to chastity and celibacy. While she seeks the company of men and enjoys being in the midst of male action and power, she bows to no man and is not swayed by love or passion.

Athena was one of the most important Olympian goddesses and had many functions. She surpassed everybody in her main domains. A master artisan who presided over arts and crafts in peacetime, she fashioned ornate and luxuriously embroidered robes for herself and her sister Hera, the Goddess of Marriage.

In battle, Athena was known for her ferocity, but unlike her brother Ares, the God of War, she never displayed hotheadedness. She always believed in fighting for justice and righteousness, and only took part in wars that were fought in self-defence. She was unparalleled in planning, tactics, strategy and the intelligent art of war. All the Greek heroes asked for her help and advice. During the Trojan war, she inspired Odysseus and Epeios to build a wooden device in the shape of a horse, with which the Greeks gained entry to the city of Troy.

Athena is usually depicted as majestic, stern and beautiful, emanating power and authority. She is the only Olympian Goddess portrayed in armour — wearing a crested helmet, a long spear in one hand, with an aegis, or shield, over the other arm. Her favoured animals were the owl, symbolizing wisdom, and intertwined serpents, symbolizing creativity and wisdom. The olive tree, Athena's special gift to Athens, was sacred to her.

Athena was born in most unusual circumstances. Her mother Metis was Zeus's first wife. Fearing that he would be overthrown by his next child, Zeus swallowed Metis, who was already pregnant with Athena. When the time came for birth, Zeus felt tremendous headaches. As even he couldn't bear the pain, his son Hephaestus, the God of Blacksmiths and Fire, struck him with his axe. Athena leapt out of Zeus's head, fully grown and fully armed, emitting a mighty war cry. Zeus was delighted. Athena became her father's favourite child, the only one he trusted with his fabled weapon, the thunderbolt.

Athena is protector, adviser, patron, ally of heroic men, innovator, credited with introducing many useful inventions like the ship, chariot, yoke and plough, rake, bridle, trumpet and flute. She is respected for her ethical character and rational thinking, and for using her intelligence and reason to promote law, order and justice in the courts and society.

Athena archetype: Sage (Wise Woman, Warrior, Artisan)

Athena embodies the confident woman ruled by her head rather than her heart. The diversity of archetypes associated with this Goddess are a reflection of her domains. Although one Athena archetype may be more dominant, the behaviour patterns manifested in Athena women more often reflect a combination of archetypes.

The archetypes of Wisdom — the Sage archetype, the Wise Woman and Crone archetypes, and the Guide archetype — are variations on the theme of wisdom. Women embodying the Wisdom archetype are sensible, shrewd and down-to-earth. The Sage archetype encourages discipline, the pursuit of knowledge, strategy, objectivity, proximity to power and being goal oriented.

The Sage archetypes constantly seek the truth, unwilling to settle for anything but what is right and true. They thrive on knowledge, see the world objectively and always analyse details. They are dedicated to spreading the truth, and their word choice is always well considered. They are great advisers and see patterns where others may not. It is the Sage archetype that drives women towards self-reflection in the search for illumination and wisdom. Sages can be found among scholars, mentors, scientists, teachers, lawyers, journalists, politicians and philosophers.

Another powerful Athena archetype is the Warrior. The Warrior archetype is independent, focused, ambitious, assertive, goal-oriented, self-sufficient and strategic. She feels whole unto herself, usually relating to men as companions, colleagues or allies. While family and community are important to her, she is also content to be on her own. She will always gravitate towards professions that enable her to be autonomous, without having to answer to anyone else.

The Warrior archetype seeks her own counsel, often dedicating her life to championing a cause that she is passionate about. She is grounded and connected to her own source of power and claims her space in the world with confidence and an air of sovereignty. She trusts herself completely.

A Warrior archetype has a solid relationship with her own inner masculinity rather than needing an outer relationship to feel fulfilled. She is strategic and helps others to set up and maintain safe boundaries. She will not tolerate anyone disrespecting her or her loved ones, humiliating her, or trying to make her subservient. The Warrior archetype empowers women to contribute to the wellbeing of humanity and the planet through their individual gifts. Warriors can be found in the military, policing, firefighting, science, medicine and the law.

Artisan archetypes represent the essence of creativity and invention. They have fertile imaginations, like to explore new perspectives and realize their ideas in interesting and tangible forms. They are often drawn to professions where they can work with the invention, design and construction of new products, new styles and methods. Artisans lead in architecture, building, arts, technology, entertainment and fashion. Many great actors have Artisan archetypes, as acting provides a vehicle for exploring other ways of being.

Artisan archetypes do best when they are left alone to do their work. They prefer to be in their own element, deeply focusing on their task because they know that is what the world needs. Artisans can make almost anything a canvas for their creative explorations, and always in their own unique and inventive way.

Light: truth seeker, wise, articulate, open-minded, focused, ambitious, assertive, competitive, goal-oriented, self-sufficient, strong, courageous, creative, inventive, innovative, ingenious

Shadow: pedantic, critical, dogmatic, fixed, rigid in ideas, judgmental, bossy, self-absorbed, emotional passivity, moody, depressed, insular

Athena in others

The examples chosen to represent Athena — Coco Chanel, Queen Elizabeth II, Margaret Thatcher, Angela Merkel and Amal Clooney — are logical, disciplined, confident women who reflect the diversity of archetypes associated with this Goddess. They are all independent, intelligent, strategic and wise — powerful women, often perfectionists, who are dedicated to duty and truth, and resolute in championing their cause or their raison d'être.

Coco Chanel (1883–1971)

French fashion designer Gabrielle Chanel, most famously known as Coco Chanel, was a much-revered style icon, famous for her timeless designs, trademark suits, little black dresses and sophisticated ensembles. An Artisan archetype, Coco embodied the essence of modern, cutting-edge creativity, invention and innovation. For her, 'fashion is not something that exists in dresses only. Fashion is in the sky, in the street, fashion has to do with ideas, the way we live, what is happening'.

Coco's early years were impoverished. After her mother died, she was placed in an orphanage by her father. There, the nuns taught her to sew — a skill that led to her career.

By strategically building alliances with wealthy, aristocratic men friends, Coco opened her first shop and started out selling hats. Other stores followed. In the 1920s she launched her first perfume, Chanel No. 5, the first to feature a designer's name. It remains today a must-have perfume. To Coco, 'perfume is the unseen, unforgettable, ultimate accessory of fashion … that heralds your arrival and prolongs your departure'.

In 1925, Coco introduced the stylish Chanel suit with collarless jacket and well-fitted skirt. Her designs were revolutionary for the time and borrowed elements of menswear, like trousers, and emphasizing comfort over the constraints of then-popular fashions. Another acclaimed design was her little black dress. Coco took a colour once associated with mourning and showed how chic it could be for evening wear.

Like Athena, Coco never married or had children. She also manifested many other Athena traits — she was wise, a perfectionist, ambitious and strategic. She understood well the value of proximity to power to achieve her ambitions, but without sacrificing her independence. Coco believed, 'the most courageous act is still to think for yourself. Aloud.'

But there was a shadow side to Coco. Her meteoric rise and prominent standing and connections helped her regain control over her life at a crucial time. After the Nazis took over Paris in 1940, Coco began sleeping with the enemy. Athena, as the Goddess of War, was thinking strategically. Her romance with an officer of the Abwehr, the German military intelligence, enabled her to move into comfortable living quarters at Paris' Hôtel Ritz, then doubling as German headquarters. It's believed Coco became an Abwehr agent in 1941.

Although reportedly outed as a spy in 1944, she escaped punishment and erased all evidence of any actions that tied her to the Abwehr. Coco never endured any adverse ramifications for her wartime dealings with the Nazis, and made a celebrated return to the fashion world in 1954.

Queen Elizabeth II (1926–)

Queen Elizabeth II of Great Britain ascended the throne in 1952, making her the longest-reigning monarch in British history. While the political and social landscape both in the United Kingdom and the world has undergone drastic upheaval and change during her reign, Elizabeth II, like Athena, has remained a popular, much loved and respected monarch, embracing the regal pomp and ceremony as part of her role as sovereign.

Like Athena, who had to acknowledge and ally herself with a higher authority in Zeus, the Queen clearly understands her powers and the scope of her role as monarch within the parliamentary and Commonwealth framework. 'I cannot lead you into battle,' she said in her first televised Christmas broadcast in 1957. 'I do not give you laws or administer justice but I can do something else — I can give my heart and my devotion to these old islands and to all the peoples of our brotherhood of nations.'

Along with her years of experience, the Wisdom archetypes are deeply embedded in Elizabeth II. The Queen is sensible and shrewd, well-known for the dignity and discretion with which she negotiates the complexity of her role with political leaders and fellow monarchs. She is admired and applauded for standing her ground and for her sense of duty. Marriage and the need to provide heirs to the throne were an expected part of that duty, and although family is important to her, duty always comes first.

Like Athena, the Queen sees public service as one of the most important elements of her work and is patron or president to many charities and organizations. She actively supports and encourages innovations and achievements in all walks of life, and strives for these contributions to society to be recognised.

> I know of no single formula for success. But over the years I have observed that some attributes of leadership are universal and are often about finding ways of encouraging people to combine their efforts, their talents, their insights, their enthusiasm and their inspiration to work together.
>
> —Queen Elizabeth II

Margaret Thatcher (1925–2013)

Margaret Thatcher was prime minister of the United Kingdom from 1979 to 1990, the longest-serving British prime minister of the twentieth century, the first woman to hold that office, and the most renowned British prime minister since Winston Churchill.

Like Athena, she represents the Sage, the woman who is ruled by her head rather than her heart. Margaret also embodied the Warrior archetype. Dubbed the Iron Lady or the Perfumed Steamroller, she strategically wielded her power and influence like a weapon to champion causes and achieve significant political change. But, because of her zealous regard for the individual over the state, her uncompromising politics and combative leadership style, the outcomes weren't always perceived to be for the good of the people. 'Do you know,' she said, 'one of the greatest problems of our age is that we are governed by people who care more about feelings than they do about thoughts and ideas? Now, thoughts and ideas, that interests me.'

Inheriting a weak economy, Margaret reduced or eliminated governmental regulations and subsidies to businesses, and privatized many state-owned industries and public services. But recession, rising unemployment and social unrest made her deeply unpopular. A decisive victory in the 1982 Falklands War brought a resurgence of support, winning her a second term in a landslide victory, in which she promised to curb the power of the unions. 'We had to fight the enemy without in the Falklands,' she said of the war. 'We always have to be aware of the enemy within, which is much more difficult to fight and more dangerous to liberty.'

In 1984 a nationwide strike of miners was called to prevent the closing of coal mines that the government claimed were unproductive. The walkout, which lasted nearly a year, was marred by violent clashes between unionists and police, and nearly brought Britain to a standstill. Resolutely, Margaret crushed them; the miners returned to work without winning a single concession. The legacy of that bitterness still lives on today. Displaying that resolution, Margaret said, 'If you lead a country like Britain, a strong country, a country which has taken a lead in world affairs in good times and in bad, a country that is always reliable, then you have to have a touch of iron about you.'

After her third electoral victory in 1987, Margaret adopted a more hostile attitude towards the idea of a European Community. Her traditionally pro-European party became divided, and a string of senior cabinet ministers resigned over the issue. The unwise implementation of a poll tax in 1989 produced outbreaks of street violence and alarmed the rank-and-file members of her party as well as those who were affected by the tax.

Spurred on by public opposition of the poll tax and Margaret's increasingly strident and divisive politics, Conservative members of parliament moved against her in November 1990, and, after her leadership was challenged, she resigned.

Although many observers saw her implacable, combative nature and divisive politics as shadow aspects of her personality, Margaret never did. To her, they were strengths, ones she believed others should emulate.

Angela Merkel (1954–)

Angela Merkel is a German scientist turned politician. She is distinguished for becoming the first female chancellor of Germany in 2005, and for being one of the architects of the European Union. Twice married, but with no children, the focus of the media spotlight has always been on her politics. Angela is Athena incarnate: a leader wielding power and influence like a weapon to champion causes and achieve change, but always for the good of the people. 'Politicians have to be committed to people in equal measures,' she once said.

Early in her career, East Germany's secret police, the Stasi, offered her a position as a spy. Angela declined, preferring to pursue a career in physics because, as the Sage in her put it, 'there, the truth isn't so easily bent'.

The fall of the Berlin Wall in November 1989 served as the catalyst for Angela's political career. She became involved in the growing democracy movement and joined the new party, the Christian Democratic Union, a party committed to steering the peaceful and democratic reunification of Germany.

During her fourth term in government, Angela was seen as the *de facto* leader of Europe, presiding over the region's largest economy, having steered Germany through financial crises and back to growth. She championed austerity as the path to recovery for Europe's endangered economies. Faced with Europe's gravest refugee crisis and humanitarian emergency since World War II, Angela resolved that Germany would keep its borders open, because to her, 'when it comes to human dignity, we cannot make compromises'.

Angela's leadership was characterized by a steely reserve and the boldness of her decisions. She stood up to then US president Donald Trump, and allowed more than a million Syrian refugees into Germany because she believed it was the right thing to do. A 2020 survey found 75 per cent of adults in fourteen European countries trusted Angela Merkel more than any other leader in the region. She topped the *Forbes* list of the most powerful women in the world every year since 2006 with the exception of 2010, which went to American First Lady, Michelle Obama.

Like Athena, Angela is respected and admired for her ethical character and rational thinking, and for using her intelligence and reason to promote law, order and justice. A rare honour for a politician in the modern world.

> You could certainly say that I've never underestimated myself, there's nothing wrong with being ambitious.
> —Angela Merkel

Amal Alamuddin Clooney (1978–)

Lebanese–British attorney and activist Amal Alamuddin Clooney specializes in international law and human rights issues. Amal embodies both the Sage and the Warrior archetype.

Born in Beirut, Amal was a toddler when her family fled Lebanon to escape the ravages of the violent civil war that had engulfed the country. The family settled in London. With the Sage in her to the fore, Amal was an excellent student, earning a scholarship to the University of Oxford. While there, she developed an interest in human rights, before graduating in law.

Amal moved to New York to complete her studies. After passing the bar, she worked with one of the world's top-ranked law firms before refocusing her career on international law and moving back to London's Doughty Street Chambers, a firm with a history of human rights work.

The Warrior archetype in Amal is evident when she is defending government leaders who were imprisoned for the wrong reasons, and when she powerfully advocates on behalf of neglected and exploited groups, pursuing justice for persecuted peoples and countries. Beyond her criminal defence cases, Amal has held several important advisory roles, including working for the United Nations on counterterrorism and, in particular, detailing human rights violations of women. She believes, 'holding back women is holding back half of every country in the world'.

Outside court, Amal lectures on criminal law at institutions such as the University of London and the Hague Academy of International Law and serves as a visiting faculty member at Columbia Law School. Like Athena, Amal is renowned for her intelligent leadership and skill, her commitment to justice and her strategic ability to handle complex and difficult criminal cases and proceedings.

Like many Athena women, Amal gravitates towards successful men, but was convinced she would remain unmarried. A surprise marriage proposal from George Clooney, a rich and powerful American actor and director, changed her mind. Children followed for the politically minded power couple, but this Athenian Goddess remains passionately committed to the cause of human rights and the wellbeing of humanity.

> Be courageous. Challenge orthodoxy. Stand up for
> what you believe in. When you are in your rocking
> chair talking to your grandchildren many years
> from now, be sure you have a good story to tell.
> —Amal Alamuddin Clooney

Other examples of Athena

Eleanor Roosevelt, Nancy Wake, Maya Angelou, Kamala Harris

Reflections on the Athena in you

Do you recognize the Goddess Athena in you?

Is the Sage an archetype you strongly identify with?

How long has she been in you?

List the ways Athena manifests in you.

What gifts does the Athena in you bring?

Any shadows?

Who are some other women who embody the Goddess Athena?

6

Hestia

Goddess of The Hearth, Home and Hospitality

Archetype: Spiritual Seeker

The psyches and souls of women also have their own cycles and seasons of doing and solitude, running and staying, being involved and being removed, questing and resting, creating and incubating, of being of the world and returning to the soul-place.

—Clarissa Pinkola Estés, *Women Who Run with the Wolves*

Hestia mythology

Hestia was the Greek Goddess of the Hearth, Home and Hospitality. Her Roman counterpart was Vesta. The eldest daughter of Titans Cronus and Rhea, her siblings were Zeus, Poseidon, Hades, Hera and Demeter.

Hestia was one of three independent or virgin Goddesses; the other two being her nieces, Athena and Artemis. When the gods Apollo and Poseidon courted her, she refused to marry, wanting to remain chaste forever. Zeus, the king of the gods, then granted her the leading place of presiding over all sacrifices.

This Goddess was the personification of the hearth, protector of the family and political community. In ancient Greece, the worship of Hestia was an integral part of life. Sacrifices and offerings were regularly made to the Goddess in Athens, whether it was at the family hearth, the city's public hearth, or in the temples of the Gods, where each one had their own hearth. By tradition, as Zeus had decreed, Hestia received a share of every sacrifice, and before other gods, even at such places as Olympia, where Zeus was honoured.

Family members gathered around the hearth, the focal point for many activities. It symbolized the heart and soul of the home, and was not just for cooking or warmth. When a family member left their home to begin a new family, a parcel of fire was taken to begin the new home fire — symbolizing the continuity of family.

Each town centre also had its communal hearth where the public fire was maintained. The fire of the Hestia, meaning the hearth, was also used in sacrifices, therefore taking on a sacred character to its citizens. The Goddess was believed to be the divine representation of tranquillity in domestic life.

Hestia voluntarily relinquished her place among the Gods on Mount Olympus, swapping with Dionysus. She preferred to withdraw from godly affairs and the other Gods because of their all-too-human weaknesses, jealous wrangling, disputes and wars. As Goddess of the Hearth, Home and Hospitality, Hestia could always count on a warm welcome in any city she chose to visit.

Hestia archetype: Spiritual Seeker (Hermit, Homebody, Mystic)

As Hestia is the hearth in the home, it is the centring fire that makes every home a temple and sacred place. While the Artemis and Athena archetypes were externally oriented, the Hestia archetypes are introverted, focused on their inner world and inner wisdom.

The Hestia archetype's focus is for herself. She embodies the grounded wise woman who finds comfort in solitude and exudes a sense of wholeness. Unlike Athena and Artemis, Hestia shied away from the world and the wilderness; her domain remained indoors, centred around the hearth.

A Hestia archetype today may prefer to live a more solitary life, or live within a community of like-minded spiritual sisters, or when such isolation is not possible, to set aside periods of time from a busy lifestyle for herself. Me time — time with which to embrace solitude in order to refresh, rejuvenate, renew or to just rest and relax.

While each of the Artemis and Athena archetypes has a distinct and diverse personality type and role, the Hestia archetypes are all similarly inner-focused and inner directed; the distinction between Spiritual Seeker, Hermit, Homebody or Mystic archetypes is more a matter of degree.

Spiritual Seeker archetypes project warmth, security, reflectiveness, a sense of accomplishment and contentment within themselves. They seek peace and harmony, which for them is most easily found in solitude. They constantly seek insight into who they are, give priority to spiritual understanding and want more from life than material success.

Spiritual Seeker archetypes are not necessarily religious. Most often, they have little interest in organized religious practice, preferring to follow a path of self-discovery or transformation; like a butterfly that wants to spread its wings, to learn and experience more. The Spiritual Seeker is the archetypal energy that gives us the motivation to travel the world, to change careers, to find new ventures, understand new philosophies or to write books or poetry.

Many artists, musicians, writers and poets are seekers of transformation. Their work taps into a deeper sense of knowing, and conveys underlying messages that can move, change and/or offer hope of something better. Everyone embodies the Spiritual Seeker archetype, although some people are more in tune with this dimension than others.

The Mystic archetype is an intriguing member of this family, bringing us into the world of the soul. Mysticism can be found in all religions. Mystics search for their inner compass through deep spiritual reflection. They withdraw from the physical world as their life journey centres on a commitment to live in the conscious mind, body and spirit and in harmony with the truth. They pride themselves on their integrity and are often extremely humble people.

The Mystic archetype believes in a higher power, a unifying, pure, undying, omnipresent force. In the light, the Mystic brings a beautiful grace. She is a sea of tranquillity for those around her. She models virtuosity and pure devotion. She is a source of grace, divine light and divine visions — a well of faith for others to drink from.

The Hermit archetype is associated with physical and social isolation. Someone who enjoys time on their own to think and create. Every Hermit has their own hermitage, a psychic cocoon they can escape to. We all encounter the Hermit at some stage in our lives. When we withdraw from the world after a devastating trauma, when suffering a bereavement, losing a job, or falling ill. This hermitage, or inner sanctum, is often our safest place.

Homebodies are a type of Hermit. A Homebody enjoys the warmth and simple pleasures of being at home — cooking, housekeeping, decorating, gardening or having friends over. The Homebody archetype savours their time alone. It's very important for them to spend quality time by themselves, cultivating their skills and interests and enjoying the comforts and tranquillity of home. Homebodies have a talent for transforming a house into a home, a sanctuary, where every minute spent feels like bliss.

Homebodies can be women who choose to spend most of their time at home, where their contentment and creativity flourishes in the peace and harmony. Or they can be women with busy, successful or high-powered careers, where spending time at home and being a Homebody is a welcome retreat from the limelight or the stress and busyness of the world.

> **Light:** confidence, deep concentration, creativity, soulful, prioritizes inner peace, tranquillity, autonomy, ambition, identity and possibility thinking, selflessness, mindfulness, wisdom, gratitude

> **Shadow:** deep introversion, social isolation, emotional frigidity, fear of being trapped, being an eternal seeker, gets so lost in the Divine, Earthly concerns are forsaken, reclusive, agoraphobic

Hestia in others

Hestia is as readily found in males as in females, and behavioural traits, such as seeking solitude, spiritual awareness or being a homebody, are likely to be a lifelong archetypal pattern.

Emily Dickinson, Rachel Denton, Margaret Fairchild, Enya and Nigella Lawson represent the varying aspects of the Hestia archetype. All are independent, inner-centred women for whom the home is their temple and their hermitage.

Emily Dickinson (1830–86)

Famed American poet Emily Dickinson was a recluse and lived much of her life in isolation. Considered an eccentric by locals, she always wore white, spoke to visitors through doors, gave treats to local children by lowering a basket from a second-storey window and refused to attend her father's funeral, instead listening to it from her bedroom.

Emily didn't leave the family property for the last two decades of her life. She never married, and most of her friendships depended entirely upon correspondence. While a prolific writer, only ten of her nearly 1800 poems and one letter were published in her lifetime.

Emily embraced most of the Hestia archetypes. She was a Spiritual Seeker and a Hermit, with a touch of the Mystic that could be attributed to her sense of higher calling and her fascination with death and the world of the soul. Unusually for a woman with her education, religious and family background and upbringing, Emily had a fierce independent and rebellious streak, and refused to be silenced, as is particularly evident in her writing and her dogged determination to not be confined by the roles expected of her.

> The Soul selects her own Society —
> Then — shuts the Door —
> To her divine Majority —
> Present no more —
> Unmoved — she notes the Chariots — pausing —

At her low Gate —
Unmoved — an Emperor be kneeling
Upon her Mat —
I've known her — from an ample nation —
Choose One —
Then — close the Valves of her attention —
Like Stone —

Like the soul of her description referred to in the poem above, the demands of her family and friends' religion prompted such desire to escape. 'Christ is calling everyone here; all my companions have answered … I am standing alone in rebellion and growing very careless.'

As an unmarried daughter, Emily was expected to demonstrate her dutiful nature by setting aside her own interests in order to meet the needs of home. Her letters from the 1850s register her increasing dislike of domestic work and frustration with the time constraints created by the household, by chores that were never done. 'God keep me,' she said, 'from what they call households.'

Emily was also ambivalent toward marriage and her perception of what the role of wife required.

The Playthings of Her Life

To take the honorable Work
Of Woman, and of Wife —

If ought She missed in Her new Day,
Of Amplitude, or Awe —

Or first Prospective — Or the Gold
In using, wear away,

It lay unmentioned — as the Sea
Develop Pearl, and Weed,
But only to Himself — be known
The Fathoms they abide

Emily believed that, for her, salvation depended on freedom. And freedom of her soul demanded withdrawal from the humdrum world into the solitary, spiritual realm of her poetry.

> Escape is such a thankful word.
> —Emily Dickinson

Rachel Denton (1963–)

For English woman Rachel Denton, the Hermit archetype has been deeply embedded all her life. 'Solitude has always been important to me,' she has said.

Growing up in a crowded Catholic household, what Rachel valued most was being able to play in her room alone. Becoming a nun appealed from an early age. She chose to join the Carmelite order because of its focus on solitude, but convent life was so tightly structured she found it hard to find time to be alone. She subsequently became claustrophobic and left after a year to pursue a career in teaching.

The social world of teaching also left too little time for the solitude Rachel sought. And she found that when opportunities for relationships presented themselves, she chose not to pursue them; the compulsion towards a life of silence and solitude was stronger. So Rachel purchased a cottage with a garden big enough to grow her own food and keep a few chickens, and thus founded her own one-nun hermitage in Lincolnshire, England.

'A hermit is a person who chooses to live alone, and does that with the intention of, in some sense, finding God.' Rachel made an official commitment to be a hermit in 2006 at a special mass. Her vows were poverty, chastity and obedience, which she interprets as simplicity, solitude and silence. Contact with close friends and family is maintained by phone and internet, but they understand her need for solitude, and visit only once or twice a year.

> It is not always easy to live this way; I know it could be seen as a selfish life. But having experienced the stillness and silence I have always longed for, I know that I am growing.
> —Rachel Denton

Margaret Fairchild (1911–89)

Margaret Fairchild was an English concert pianist, nun and homeless woman. The latter part of Margaret's life was portrayed in the 2015 film *The Lady in the Van*. Her character, Miss Shepherd, was played by Maggie Smith. Margaret represents the Spiritual Seeker, Hermit and Homebody archetypes and the fine line that these inner-centred archetypes tread between the light and shadow aspects of their personality, when trauma or tragedy strikes.

Margaret's brother said that the convent forced her to abandon her love of music and playing piano in order to concentrate on her faith. She left the order following a nervous breakdown. Because of her increasingly erratic behaviour, her brother committed her to a psychiatric institution. While fleeing incarceration, the van Margaret was driving hit and killed a motorcyclist. Margaret mistakenly believed that she was responsible for his death. By the late 1960s, Margaret, under the assumed name of Mary Sheppard, was living in a van, on the run, and in perpetual fear of being arrested.

She chose to park outside the affluent houses in Gloucester Crescent, Camden Town, whereupon after annoying homeowners with the build-up of rubbish bags around the van, she would be asked to move on. Sometime later, she ended up parked outside writer Alan Bennett's house. Because she was often terrorized by passers-by, but also because of the interruptions that Margaret, or Miss Sheppard as he knew her, caused to his work, he allowed her to move her van from the street into his driveway. After her van was in his drive for a time, she took up squatters' rights and would not, and could not, be moved.

Margaret was difficult. She was eccentric, poor and homeless. From time to time, local nuns would bring her food to supplement what she bought with her social security payments, though she did not have means of cooking in the van; nor did she have a toilet. Bennett ran an electric cable from his house to the van so she could run a heater and a television.

Margaret's van was her home, her haven from a heartless world. She lived in her van in Bennett's driveway for fifteen years until her death in 1989. It was only then that he learnt from her brother who Miss Sheppard really was.

Enya (1961–)

Enya, Irish singer, songwriter and musician, is Hestia personified. She has sold 75 million albums worldwide, won four Grammys, been nominated for an Oscar for her music on the *Lord of The Rings* soundtrack, and holds the title of the richest woman in British and Irish music history, yet she has never toured as a solo artist. Instead, Enya spends her days a recluse in her castle in Dublin and has only been spotted in public twice in ten years.

Following a split from her family band Clannad at age 21, Enya started writing music with Nicky Ryan (Clannad's producer) and his wife Roma, which led to the release of their first album. But it was their second LP, *Watermark*, that put them on the map, with 'Orinoco Flow (Sail Away)' selling 11 million copies worldwide. Their success continues to this day.

There is no one else in the music business who is so successful yet about whom so little is known. Enya doesn't socialize; she's barely seen out of the house. Even her family hardly ever sees her. She rarely performs live and only then in small, intimate gigs. Why? 'I am really a very shy person,' she says. 'If I appear, it is because of the music, not because I want to be seen.'

Enya embodies the independence of Hestia, living life on her terms, withdrawn from the world at large, isolated from people yet still connected via the haunting sounds of her transformative music. The Spiritual Seeker and Hermit archetypes are starkly to the fore in this brilliant musician. Music is her first and present love.

> I don't need a man in my life ... My affairs are with melody and words and beautiful sounds. I'm too much devoted to my music. Some people think it sounds sad but believe me, I'm happy. I am my music.
> —Enya

Nigella Lawson (1960–)

Nigella Lawson is an English broadcaster, journalist, television personality, cook and food writer who hosts her own cooking shows. Nigella is a Goddess of the Hearth, Home and Hospitality personified.

The Hestia in her reaches out in her latest book, *Cook, Eat, Repeat*. Nigella believes that many of us have become alienated from the domestic sphere, and it can make us feel better to reclaim that space and make it comforting rather than frightening. To her, 'baking is a useful metaphor for the warmth of the kitchen, and a way of reclaiming our lost Eden'.

Nigella's is the kind of cooking that cuts through things, and to things, which have nothing to do with the kitchen. She shows that the mundane has the potential to take us to another, more comforting place. Which is why it matters. 'Sometimes,' she wrote in her book, *How to be a Domestic Goddess*, 'we don't want to feel like a postmodern, postfeminist, overstretched woman but, rather, a domestic Goddess, trailing nutmeggy fumes of baking pie in our languorous wake.'

What Nigella is talking about is not exactly being a domestic Goddess, but feeling like one. To her, and to many others who embrace the Hestia archetype, this is what baking is all about: feeling good, wafting along in the warm, sweet-smelling air, unwinding, no longer being entirely an office creature; becoming immersed in comfort cooking and the nurturing generosity of hospitality. Allowing the inner peace, harmony, comfort and safety of the rituals of the hearth of Hestia to seep into the heart and mind. Finding one's soul space.

> I think we all live in a world that is so fast-paced, it's threatening and absolutely saturated with change and novelty and insecurity. Therefore, the ritual of cooking and feeding my family and friends, whoever drops in, is what makes me feel that I'm in a universe that is contained.
>
> —Nigella Lawson, *How to Be a Domestic Goddess*

Other examples of Hestia

Hildegarde of Bingen, Harper Lee, Mary Berry, Adele

Reflections on the Hestia in you

Do you recognize the Goddess Hestia in you?

Is the Spiritual Seeker an archetype you strongly identify with?

How long has Hestia been in you?

List the ways Hestia manifests in you.

What gifts does the Hestia in you bring?

Any shadows?

Who are some other women who embody the Goddess Hestia?

7

Hera

Goddess of Marriage, Queen of the Gods

Archetype: Wife, Queen

There was no harassing restraint, no repressing of glee
and vivacity, with him; for with him I was at perfect ease,
because I knew I suited him; all I said or did seemed either
to console or revive him. Delightful consciousness! It
brought to life and light my whole nature; in his presence
I thoroughly lived, and he lived in mine.

—Charlotte Brontë, *Jane Eyre*

Hera mythology

Hera was the Olympian Queen of the Gods, and the Goddess of Marriage. Born after Hestia and Demeter, Hera is the youngest daughter of Titans Cronus and Rhea, and the sister and wife of Zeus. Her Roman counterpart was Juno.

Hera was worshipped throughout the Greek world, first as Queen of Heaven, consort of Zeus, King of the Gods and Supreme Ruler and, second, as the Goddess of Marriage. As such, she is the deity most associated with family and was the protector of women, presiding over marriages and birth.

Hera symbolizes regal power and beauty. She is confident and in command of her world, often depicted as a beautiful woman wearing a crown and holding a royal, lotus-tipped sceptre. Hera's sacred animal was the cow. Her sacred bird was first the cuckoo, and later the peacock.

Zeus tricked Hera into marriage. After he attempted, unsuccessfully, to court her, he disguised himself as a shivering little cuckoo to obtain pity from her. His ruse worked. When Hera picked up the bird and fondly held it to her breast, Zeus morphed into his true shape and raped her. Hera was shamed into marrying him.

It wasn't a happy marriage for the Queen of the Gods. Zeus was brutish and cruel to everybody. As Hera's husband, he shamed her by engaging in numerous extramarital sexual liaisons, causing her further humiliation. However, with resolute courage and self-belief, and incapable of bearing the victimisation any longer, Hera stood up to the tyrant by plotting a revenge plan with Poseidon and Athena. After drugging Zeus, they tied him to his bed and stole his thunderbolt.

Zeus, when subsequently freed, was so angry he hung Hera from the clouds with golden chains and attached heavy anvils to her feet. In order to be released, Hera swore to never rebel against her husband again. Instead, she became jealous and vindictive, directing her anger toward Zeus's lovers and their offspring instead.

Despite her notorious and heartless ferocity towards Zeus' love interests, Hera publicly epitomized the sacred values of marriage and complemented her male counterpart, Zeus, well, with her divine presence, command and authority.

Hera archetype: Wife, Queen

Hera belongs in the Relational Goddess category. She is relationship-oriented and therefore vulnerable. Relational archetypes encompass the traditional roles of women whose identity, sense of purpose, meaning and wellbeing depend on whether they are in a significant relationship. The personification of the traits of wife, mother and daughter leads to an inherent vulnerability in their roles because of their dependence on others to satisfy their needs. The Hera archetype's status and power, as well as much of her identity, can only be realized if it is connected to a partner.

Hera represents the feminine archetype of wife and matriarch of the family, the union of the masculine and the feminine. She is a Goddess devoted to commitment and partnership and thrives in the union of marriage. The Wife archetype needs the respect, prestige and honour that marriage promises her. Her instinct is to marry and build meaningful alliances. She considers her other roles — whether student, career woman or mother — secondary to her essential goal of finding a partner and being married.

The Wife archetype represents the capacity to be committed, bonded, loyal and to endure difficulties with a partner. A Hera woman enjoys making her partner the centre of her life, with an expectation that they will fulfil her needs, and believes that both she and her partner are continually transformed by marriage.

But becoming a wife and having a family has always been a pervasive cultural stereotype for women, and these societal expectations are sometimes more powerful influencers of behaviour than the archetypes. Therefore, just as a Hera archetype feels incomplete without a partner, many single women are enticed into the storybook notion of marriage and family, and may find themselves living roles that are at odds with how they truly think and feel.

Due to devotion to the union of marriage, the Hera woman has the ability to unite people and is a manifestation of what it means to be loyal and committed to a relationship or cause. Additionally, she possesses the ability to care and endure.

In her role as mother and matriarch, the archetypal Hera acts selflessly, with devotion and care to those in life whom she values, even to her own cost, in order to protect those she loves. However, if the Hera archetype feels the family unit is threatened, she can display anger, rage or jealousy or take revenge, either against her partner or the others involved.

For a woman with the Wife archetype, being single or childless can be difficult and deeply painful, but her biggest challenge is overcoming her jealousy, vindictiveness or inability to leave a destructive relationship. Once a Hera woman is abused, betrayed or feels discarded, she may go to extremes for revenge.

Women with the Queen archetype are often attracted to powerful partners whose high degree of success and prestige privileges her to enjoy a position of status and power. Traditional in her values, she seeks social prestige and matriarchal rulership through marriage and, when appreciated or fulfilled, is capable of demonstrating complete loyalty to her spouse and their goals.

A Queen archetype represents the power and authority of women who rule over any domain. Symbolically, her court may be a corporation, office or home environment where everyone there answers directly to her. How she rules depends on whether her spouse acknowledges or challenges their power, how respectfully she is treated, and whether her light or shadow attributes are in the ascendancy.

In the light aspect, the Queen archetype represents the regal feminine. She rules with kindness, firmness, tolerance and mercy. She uses her benevolent authority to protect others and is adored by her people. This kind of Queen sees her own empowerment enhanced by her relationships and experience.

The shadow aspect reflects the tendency to become arrogant, controlling, defensive and aggressive when challenged. The shadow Queen can slip into cruel and destructive patterns of behaviour, particularly when she perceives that her authority or capacity to maintain control over her court is being challenged. Or when betrayed, the Queen can become detached, indifferent to the genuine needs of others — whether material or emotional.

> **Light:** self-assurance, self-belief, devotion, loyalty, commitment, faithful, strength, courage, determination, protectiveness, authority
>
> **Shadow:** arrogant, controlling, angry, jealous, possessive, vindictive, manipulative, destructive, defensive, needy, obsessive, indifferent

Hera in others

Hera is one of the most powerful and respected Goddesses. But because her status is indelibly intertwined with that of her partner, and because of the public nature of her marriage, she is vulnerable. The more famous the couple, the more media scrutiny and speculation they attract, and the greater potential for a shadow to be cast over the marriage, and the personality, especially the wife's. This is exemplified in the women who personify Hera — Jacqueline Kennedy Onassis, Camilla, Duchess of Cornwall, Ellen DeGeneres, Victoria Beckham, Hillary Clinton and Lorena Bobbitt.

Jacqueline Kennedy Onassis (1929–94)

Former American first lady Jacqueline Kennedy, noted for her style and elegance, personifies the Hera archetypes of Wife and Queen. She knew destiny was calling when her husband, John F. Kennedy, was elected president of the United States of America. But according to her priorities, 'I'll be a wife and mother first, then first lady'.

Although Jackie's marriage to Jack was a love match, it strengthened the Kennedy dynasty and aided the family's rise to political power. When she became first lady her own personal power and prestige was further enhanced. For three years the Kennedys lived a life of glamour, power and idealism that was unprecedented in American politics.

But like Zeus, her husband had a weakness for other women and was known for his promiscuity and frequent infidelities, often flaunting his mistresses in front of her. Unlike Hera, Jackie appeared to be able to accept this as a normal part of the world of marriage, men and power, and turned a blind eye. 'I don't think there are any men who are faithful to their wives,' she once said. Protecting her children and family was more important, and seen as part of her duty as wife and queen.

Jacqueline Kennedy created her own unique role and style, becoming one of the most loved and fabled first ladies in American history, and one of the most admired and respected women in the world. Her most enduring contribution was her dedication to restoring the White House to its original elegance and to protect, preserve and expand its historical holdings.

After John F. Kennedy's assassination in 1963, Jackie knew it was not only the end of an era, but the end of their realm. To save and protect JFK's legacy and her own, the former first lady created a myth, likening their court to the romance, honour and integrity of the reign of King Arthur: 'There'll be great presidents again, but there'll never be another Camelot ... It will never be that way again.'

When her brother-in-law, Bobby Kennedy, on whom she had always leant for moral support, was gunned down in 1968, Jackie feared for her life and the lives of her children. Soon after she married again, attracted by another powerful man, wealthy Greek shipping tycoon, Aristotle (Ari) Onassis. The dominant Hera within had asserted the need to become Wife and Queen again, but this time in a very different realm.

Onassis offered security. He owned Skorpios, his own island in Greece, a private army and an airline. He could give her anything she wanted, including protection. But despite the affluent lifestyle, the marriage soon soured. Ari began seeing his old flame, opera singer Maria Callas, again. Subsequently, Jackie spent more and more time in New York, and they lived mostly separate lives. If Ari hadn't died, they would most likely have divorced. From his will, Jackie received US$26 million while his daughter, Christina Onassis, inherited the bulk of her father's US$500 million estate.

Some archetypes, like Hera, are more dominant at certain phases of a woman's life. As women age, these archetypes sometimes become less influential. This was evident in Jackie's last love, Maurice Tempelsman. The wealthy diamond trader was her soulmate and third husband in all but legal terms, for the last decade of her life.

> The first time you marry for love, the second for money, and the third for companionship.
>
> —Jacqueline Kennedy Onassis

Camilla, Duchess of Cornwall (1947–)

In the ultra-conservative world of the British monarchy, the marriage of Camilla, Duchess of Cornwall, to Prince Charles, heir to the throne, was a triumph against the odds. Theirs was a love and union of souls that had endured for decades and had exposed vulnerabilities and weaknesses in each other, and in the royal family. They inevitably became enmeshed and engulfed in the scandals and tragic consequences of their love affair.

Eventual marriage to Charles brought a happy ending to their love story. It also legitimized their alliance and brought Camilla recognition, respectability and respite from the condemnation and vilification for being the other woman when Charles was married to the immensely popular and beautiful Princess Diana. Now, Camilla has her man and an increasingly prominent royal role to play. As the rightful wife of the next British king, Camilla is finally in her court.

The Hera archetype is a dominant part of Camilla's make-up. Her relationship with Prince Charles began in 1970, but she was considered a commoner and too experienced with men to be considered a suitable match for the future king. Camilla then married and had two children with Andrew Parker Bowles.

Like most other English girls with her background, she'd been raised to expect that her life path would be marriage, then a home with husband and children. Charles was devastated, but was encouraged to marry a more suitable partner, Lady Diana Spencer, with whom he later had two sons. Throughout, Camilla and Charles remained close friends and confidants.

As both their marriages became unhappy and troubled, their love affair reignited. Charles finally publicly admitted to committing adultery with Camilla and she divorced in 1995. A year later, Charles and Diana divorced. However, Camilla still wasn't seen as suitable for the prince. She was unpopular with members of the royal family and the public. In the eyes of many, she was an adulteress who had wreaked havoc on Princess Diana's life and marriage. Camilla and Charles recognized this, and included this prayer of penitence in their wedding ceremony: 'We acknowledge and bewail our manifold sins and wickedness, which we, from time to time, most grievously have committed, by thought, word and deed, against thy divine majesty, provoking most justly thy wrath and indignation against us. We do earnestly repent, and are heartily sorry for these misdoings.'

The second time around, Camilla and Charles were resolute, unwilling to give each other up again. After the death of Princess Diana, they gradually started appearing in public together, Camilla making more high-profile appearances alongside Charles, even holding hands, and the pair eventually persuaded the world, the Queen, the royal family and the establishment to accept them as a couple. When they married in 2005, Camilla not only had her longstanding soulmate as her husband, but like Hera, she now had legitimate status and prestige within the royal hierarchy, as the Duchess of Cornwall.

The strength of the Hera archetype in Camilla is evident in her preparedness to wait in the shadows for so long, to endure being treated harshly by the public, having her reputation ruined, but loving her man and dreaming of marriage and legitimacy all the while.

> I sometimes think to myself, 'Who is this woman? It can't possibly be me.' And that's really how you survive.
>
> —Camilla, Duchess of Cornwall

Ellen DeGeneres (1958–)

Ellen DeGeneres is an American comedian, television host, actress, writer and producer. She began a relationship with actress Portia de Rossi in 2004. They married shortly after California legalized same-sex marriage.

Because of her very public and powerful persona and career, Ellen represents both the Wife and Queen archetypes. For Portia, dating and then marrying one of the most famous gay women in the world came with a lot of attention, and leading such a public life was quite daunting.

In spite of the fact their private life is a source of constant speculation in the media, the marriage of this glamorous Hollywood power couple has endured for thirteen years, and against the odds, with Ellen acknowledging, 'Being her wife is the greatest thing I am.'

Homosexuality was decriminalized in the United States in 2003, but same sex marriages weren't legalized in all 50 US states until 2015. So Ellen's decision to come out in 1997, a topic rarely spoken about publicly, was courageous, provocative and inspiring; a leadership decision about claiming her right to have a wife and family of her choosing.

Ellen came out as a lesbian both in real life, when she spoke to talk show Goddess Oprah Winfrey, and then when playing her own character in the sitcom *Ellen*, she came out as gay. One of the earliest celebrities to make such a bold move, it sent shockwaves through Hollywood, the media and American audiences. The revelation was ripe tabloid fodder and often the focus of seedy gossip and commentary. Although Ellen's career suffered for a while, the Queen of daytime television was reborn and has been a respected and leading light for the LGBTQI+ community for 24 years.

Like Hera, Ellen and Portia remain committed to the ideal of marriage. California's initial legalisation and then ban on gay marriage reverberated throughout the country. For Ellen and Portia, like many other LGBTQI+ couples, establishing their relationship in the eyes of the law was vital. For Ellen, marriage was everything. And still is.

> We're together all the time. We genuinely love each other. Her happiness is my happiness, and vice versa. True love is caring more about the other person's happiness than your own.
>
> —Ellen DeGeneres

Victoria Beckham (1974–)

As thoroughly modern British celebrity power couple, Victoria and David Beckham, became husband and wife a single dove was released as a symbol of their love. Now married for 22 years, Victoria and David, nicknamed Posh and Becks, are considered by many to be the alternative British royalty, with the Hertfordshire mansion they bought after their marriage dubbed 'Beckingham Palace' by the media.

Their marriage has been lived out under the glare of the public spotlight and examined microscopically. But they appear to be a happy, devoted and busy couple sharing the raising of four children. Victoria and David pride themselves on their ability to protect their children from the limelight, keep their love burning after years of scrutiny, and support one another, often across different time zones. 'We're very present in the kids' lives,' said Victoria. 'We love our family, everything we do revolves around them.'

A pillar of Victoria and David's marriage is that it is based on merging two very high-profile, successful and lucrative careers, Victoria as a Spice Girls pop star and renowned fashion designer, and David as a professional footballer. In the early phase of their marriage, two women claimed they had had affairs with Victoria's handsome husband. Irrespective of all the allegations, Victoria stood by David and her marriage.

Since retiring, David has continued to live his life in the public eye and has been involved in a variety of projects, both charitable and commercial. Victoria has focused on her international career as a fashion designer and style idol. But unlike many marriages, whenever Victoria is away from home due to work, David is there. 'I have the support of an incredible husband. We really are equal to everything we do at home with the children. When I'm away he's the one doing the school run and doing the cooking.'

Victoria embodies the archetypes of both Wife and Queen. She believes in marriage and has achieved power and acclaim in both roles. Posh and Becks have built an empire together. Their commitment and partnership have thrived. Despite concerns about what their marriage will be like after their children have flown the coop, Victoria continues to defy rumours and find love, happiness and strength in her union with her mate.

> He's my soulmate. He's the most incredible husband.
> We complement each other. He inspires me every
> day, with the children, with the way he treats me;
> it just works. We are lucky to have each other.
> —Victoria Beckham

The shadow side of Hera can emerge when a wife feels extreme provocation or betrayal. Reactions to the stress, shame, hurt, humiliation and trauma are often a mixture of physiological, psychological, emotional, melancholic and, sometimes, monstrous actions.

According to the Healthline website, 'the fight-flight-freeze response is the body's natural reaction to danger, to a perceived threat'. While the fight-flight-freeze response causes physiological reactions, it is triggered by psychological fear. But it is not a conscious decision. It's an automatic reaction, so you can't control it; a survival instinct that our ancient forebears developed eons ago.

Hillary Clinton (1947–)

Former American first lady, Hillary Clinton, has wrestled with allegations surrounding her husband's infidelities for much of their 46-year marriage, including a sexual harassment lawsuit, a grand jury investigation and an impeachment vote based on his lying about a relationship with a White House intern.

When President Bill Clinton woke Hillary one morning to tell her that the allegations of an affair with Monica Lewinsky, a White House intern, were true, Hillary was shattered. She vividly describes her pain over the betrayal in *Living History*, her memoir. 'I could hardly breathe. Gulping for air, I started crying and yelling at him, "What do you mean? What are you saying? Why did you lie to me?" I was furious and getting more so by the second ... As a wife, I wanted to wring Bill's neck.'

Hillary came close to leaving him, but she had always loved Bill, and always believed he loved her. Like Hera, she believed in their marriage, their relationship, their parenting of daughter, Chelsea, and their shared life. But she also believed in her political future.

> The most difficult decisions I have made in my life were to stay married to Bill and to run for the Senate from New York.
>
> —Hillary Clinton, *Living History*

Lorena Bobbit (1970–)

Sometimes, a husband's provocation can become too much for a wife, as it often did with Hera, leading her to retaliate or viciously take revenge or, as in the case of Lorena Bobbitt, render her temporarily insane.

Early one morning in 1993, American woman Lorena Bobbitt, four years into her volatile marriage to John Wayne Bobbitt, took a 20-centimetre (8-inch) knife from her kitchen and cut off her husband's penis while he lay sleeping. Leaving her husband writhing in pain, Lorena drove off into the middle of nowhere and threw her husband's severed appendage into a field. She then drove to a friend's house and allowed her to call the police, offering a rough description of the location where she thought the penis had come to rest. John's severed penis was recovered from the field and miraculously reattached after lengthy surgery.

Lorena alleged that her husband had physically and emotionally abused her throughout their marriage, and had raped her the night of the attack. The verdict of the jury was not guilty by reason of temporary insanity.

Since then, Lorena, who now uses her maiden name Gallo, has evolved into an advocate for survivors of domestic violence. She lives with a partner of more than 20 years, but, because of her headline-making marriage to her first husband, Lorena has no interest in remarrying.

Other examples of Hera

Queen Elizabeth the Queen Mother, Nicole Kidman, Lily Tomlin, Catherine, Duchess of Cambridge

Reflections on the Hera in you

Do you recognize the Goddess Hera in you?

Is the Wife or Queen an archetype you strongly identify with?

How long has she been in you?

List the ways Hera manifests in you.

What gifts does the Hera in you bring?

Any shadows?

Who are some other women who embody the Goddess Hera?

8

Demeter

Goddess of the Grain, Harvest and Fertility

Archetype: Mother, Nurturer

There's something really empowering about going, 'Hell, I can do this! I can do this all!' That's the wonderful thing about mothers, you can because you must, and you just *do*. Having children just puts the whole world into perspective. Everything else just disappears.

—Kate Winslet

Demeter mythology

Demeter is the Greek Goddess of the Grain, Harvest and Fertility. Her Roman counterpart was Ceres. The other domains she presided over were Sacred Law and the Cycle of Life and Death. Demeter was the second of six children to Cronus and Rhea, born after Hestia. Her grandmother was Gaia, the Great Mother. Being the Goddess of the Grain, Harvest and Fertility, she was given a high status in ancient Greek mythology.

Even though Demeter was one of the Olympian Gods, she refused to be confined to the realms of Mount Olympus. She preferred to go to the temples dedicated to her by her followers, and to live close to those who worshipped her and, in many ways, depended on her. Demeter always had a substantial following among mortals since she had the power to bless them with rich harvests; she also created the seasons that were favourable for the planting of crops.

When Hades, God of the Underworld, abducted and raped her beloved daughter Persephone and took her to the Underworld, the grieving Demeter stopped functioning. As a consequence, nothing would grow; famine threatened to destroy humankind. Zeus had no choice; he had to intervene. He struck a deal with Hades, then sent his messenger, Hermes, to the Underworld to bring Persephone back to her mother and so prevent the extinction of all life on Earth.

The deal would allow Persephone to be by her mother's side for six months of the year. Thus, the four seasons were born. In fall and winter, when Persephone was with Hades, Demeter would become depressed. Her joy on Persephone's return coincides with the fertile spring and summer months. When Persephone was by Demeter's side, the harvest was allowed to thrive.

Usually portrayed as a robed, mature woman, Demeter can be depicted as regally seated on a throne or standing with an extended hand. Sometimes she is riding a chariot containing her daughter Persephone, and who is almost always nearby. The Goddesses shared the same attributes and symbols: ears of corn, a sheaf of wheat, a sceptre, cornucopia, torch and sometimes a crown of flowers.

Demeter archetype: Mother, Nurturer

Demeter is the archetype of the mother and nurturer. This archetype embodies the desire to nurture, the compelling nature of the maternal instinct, and the way the seasons are interwoven with the rhythms and cycles of life and nature. An entire human being grows within her body as she embodies this phase. This phase is filled with strong nurturing energy, care, self-expression, patience and protection.

Demeter is a relational Goddess; she expresses the need of a woman for connection. Demeter personifies all the traits of motherhood and is motivated by the rewards of relationship, specifically with her daughter, Persephone — love, nurturing, attention, protection. Paradoxically, while this bond gives her great strength, it also the source of her greatest vulnerability.

The Mother archetype is the most common and universally recognized archetype in most cultures and civilizations. Representing the universal, idealized version of motherhood, the archetypal Mother is depicted as either the nurturing, selfless carer who protects and provides for their offspring at any cost to themselves or, more unusually, the neglectful mother who abandons her child.

Demeter represents a person's drive to provide physical, psychological emotional and spiritual sustenance for their children. The Nurturer archetype thrives when she is offering this kind of support. Demeter motivates people to nurture others, to be generous and giving, and to find satisfaction as caretakers and providers.

Demeter archetypes have a warm nature and go out of their way to make others comfortable, especially in school and work environments. They don't compete with others and may be involved with vocations that ultimately assist other vulnerable people and children. Demeter archetypes sometimes have difficulty saying no to those who seek their help, which may result in physical or emotional burnout, frustration and depression.

The Nurturer archetype is often drawn to people in need of mothering and emotional support, which may make her vulnerable to being used. At another level, it may tie up her emotional life for years, or even drain her financially.

As the giver of life, the world has high expectations for the mother to live up to; she carries a lot of pressure — archetypally as well as culturally. She is the protector and nurturer of life, with the capacity to express unconditional love, devotion and caring. The tension in the Mother archetype is the pull between her own needs, her children's needs, or others in need of her help. Her maternal instinct causes her to naturally always put her children first. For people for whom the Demeter archetype is not as dominant, the choices are less clear-cut.

Carl Jung believed that the Mother archetype exists within the psyche of all children from a young age, with babies projecting their motherly ideals onto their primary nurturer, whether or not that individual is their biological mother. He believed that the child would attach itself to that person in the way it ordinarily would to its mother.

Another interesting aspect is that children have a way of seeing the shadow aspect of the mother figure regardless of how much she tries to be (or is) a good mother. At different stages, they may start to push back, rebel and complain, but this is part of the natural order of things. For example, when chicks spread their wings and try to venture out of the nest, the Mother archetype instinctively knows the perfect timing of when to intervene, to step back, or to let go.

There are many manifestations of the Mother archetype, traditional and modern. Career or Working Mum, Mr Mom, Virgin Mother, Biological Mother, Birth Mother, Adopted Mother, Stepmother, Single Mother, Unmarried Mother, Two Mums, Neglectful/Abusive Mother, Homemaker, Helicopter Mum, School Mum, Sports Mum, Tiger Mum, Mother Figure, Earth Mother, Mother Nature.

For a person with a dominant Demeter archetype, to not fulfil her need to have a child can engender pain, shame, a sense of failure and deep psychic wounds. That is, unless the need to nurture can be sublimated in positive and alternative ways.

The power of the mother is universal. Everyone comes under the influence of the Mother, Nurturer archetype. It is embodied in the instinct to bring something new into the world, something that wasn't there before it was brought into form. To plant a seed or an idea, to fertilize it, to nurture and care for it, to watch it grow, and then to reap the harvest. In effect, to give birth.

Light: persistence, strength, patience, single-mindedness, warmth, generosity, compassion, humanity, kindness, empathy

Shadow: difficulty saying no, burnout, frustration, depression, distress, over-mothering, smothering, stubbornness, obsessiveness, uncaring

Demeter in others

Demeter personifies the Mother, Nurturer archetype. The compelling nature of the maternal instinct and accompanying desire to nurture is the most universally recognized and deeply embedded powers in all societies and cultures. The Goddess of the Grain, Harvest and Fertility finds expression in a multitude of ways as exemplified by the following women: Diana, Princess of Wales, Cat Cora, Jacinda Ardern, Valérie Bacot and Frida Kahlo.

Diana, Princess of Wales (1961–97)

Princess Diana, wife of Charles, the Prince of Wales, heir to the British throne, was the embodiment of Demeter. Diana was a thoroughly modern princess and mother, who ripped up the rule book about royal protocol and parenting. Motherhood shaped Princess Diana, just as her determination and resolve to define the lives of her two sons, Prince William and Prince Harry, shaped theirs. And in turn, the way they are shaping their children. Although she died over twenty years ago, Diana's attitudes to parenting have had a lasting impact on raising royal children.

The Mother, Nurturer archetype was deeply embedded in Princess Diana. They were as evident in her humanitarian work as in the raising of her beloved boys, who always took top priority in her life. 'I lead from the heart, not the head,' she once said.

In the past, royal children were always left at home and tended by nannies when their parents embarked on lengthy overseas tours. Not so for Diana. Nine-month-old Prince William accompanied her and Charles to Australia for their six-week tour in 1983, and thus paved a new way for future royal parents and their children.

Diana also changed the dynamic around raising royal children. Rather than relying on nannies and bodyguards, the princess took the children to school herself, participated in school events, and guaranteed they experienced the same pursuits as less privileged children. Above all, she showered them with love and affection. Prince Harry says, 'She was the best mum in the world who smothered us with love. She would just engulf you and squeeze you as tight as possible.'

Diana wanted her children to have as normal an upbringing as possible. In turn, William and Harry are dedicated to providing their children with the same love, care and attention. Prince William remembers fondly that, 'my mother cherished those moments of privacy and being able to be that mother, rather than the Princess of Wales'.

Princess Diana combined her unerring maternal instinct and willingness to break new ground in her charitable work. She embraced unfashionable humanitarian causes such as AIDS, leprosy and land mines. She reached out to those no one else would visit and touched those no one else wanted to touch. She became a champion for children who had been forgotten or the world had neglected or written off. Nearly all her charities and humanitarian endeavours focused on children.

The universal aspects of the Demeter in Diana were evident from William and Harry's very earliest years, when she exposed them to the needs, vulnerability and disadvantage of those less privileged, taking them to a homeless shelter, on private charity visits, and making them aware of her own and others' humanitarian work. And in doing so she created an awareness of her own vulnerability and importance as a loving, devoted mother, one who was also part of the modern monarchy. An awareness that lives on in her sons.

I want them to have an understanding of people's emotions, people's insecurities, people's distress, and people's hopes and dreams. I would like a monarchy that has more contact with its people.

—Diana, Princess of Wales

Cat Cora (1967–)

For American celebrity chef Cat Cora, the road to motherhood was unconventional and filled with twists and turns.

Cat has four sons with her first wife, Jennifer. The couple used a common sperm donor, and each had their eggs harvested just once. The doctor implanted Cat and Jennifer with each other's eggs. However, for the third child, Jennifer was implanted with two embryos — one of Cat's eggs as well as one of her own. Jennifer carried the first three pregnancies and Cat, the fourth.

IVF was challenging for both women; Cat suffered a miscarriage, but the couple wanted four kids. When Jennifer became pregnant with their third child, rather than wait, they decided it would be easier to raise two young babies together, almost as twins. Fortunately, Cat, implanted with Jennifer's egg, became pregnant too. The result: two more boys.

Their family of six was now complete, but not yet legal. As a same-sex couple, they each had to legally adopt their biological children in order to become their legal parents. The couple divorced in 2016.

Cat's current wife, Nicole, has two sons of her own. Now, Cat is the mother of six boys in a blended family of eight, a family she affectionately refers to as the Wolfpack.

Jacinda Ardern (1980–)

Jacinda Ardern, Prime Minister of New Zealand, recently a proud mother, is the embodiment of Demeter and the universal power of the mother. She listens to, and learns from, children. Before becoming a world leader, Jacinda worked for an international youth organization, visiting refugee and displaced children. In addressing a United Nations General Assembly in 2018, she said, 'If you ask me why I'm in politics, my answer will be simple: children. I feel a huge duty of care to the most vulnerable, and genuinely believe that our success as leaders depends on no lesser standard than the wellbeing of children.'

Since she became prime minister in 2017, Jacinda's warm and compassionate approach has been likened to her mothering of the nation. 'How great it would be for us all to have the pride of knowing that we, as a country, are one of the best countries to be a child.'

Jacinda embodies the light aspects of the Mother and Nurturer archetypes. They are a dominant feature of her personality and her *modus operandi* as a leader. 'Kindness, and not being afraid to be kind, or to focus on, or be really driven by empathy.' This is a stark contrast to the aggressive and ruthless personality traits that have been associated with many leaders for centuries. Jacinda dismisses the notions that the qualities of kindness and empathy are mutually exclusive from qualities such as assertiveness and strength in political leadership. Instead, Jacinda continues to embrace and care for New Zealanders as family. Never was this more evident than in her response to the Christchurch terrorist attack in 2019.

> They are us. Many of those who will have been directly affected by this shooting may be migrants to New Zealand, they may even be refugees here. They have chosen to make New Zealand their home, and it is their home. They are us.
>
> —Jacinda Ardern

The lengths to which women and sometimes men will go in order to protect their children is also extraordinary. Mothers can be over-protective, fiercely so, and liable to lash out if they believe their children are in danger. Motherhood can become all-consuming and override all else.

The threat of harm or loss of a child may release, in a dominant Demeter archetype, the shadow aspects of their personality, as with Persephone. This could lead to a lack of fulfilment, a sense of frustration and failure and cause lasting emotional and psychological distress.

Valérie Bacot (1980–)

After a lifetime of abuse at the hands of her husband, Frenchwoman Valérie Bacot was in June 2021 found guilty of his murder. Surprisingly, she left court a free woman, because the court acknowledged the horror and degradation she had lived with for years.

Valérie had been abused by Daniel Polette for 28 years, first when he was her stepfather, and then when he became her husband. She was twelve when Polette first raped her. He was sent to jail, but after his release he returned and continued the abuse. At seventeen, Valérie became pregnant by Polette. She was thrown out of the house by her alcoholic mother. Valérie had four children with him. Everyone in the household was subject to Polette's alcoholic rages, especially her. Certain he would kill them all, she believed all the locals knew he was violent, but nobody said or did anything. The children tried twice to report the abuse to the *gendarmes*, but were told to go away. It was their mother's responsibility to report the abuse herself.

Valérie had nowhere to go, nobody to turn to, no money and was under Polette's control; she had no idea how to escape her daily terror of threats and violence. For years, he forced her to prostitute herself with other men, and repeatedly threatened her with a pistol, telling her he would kill her and their children if she left him. She finally snapped when he started questioning their fourteen-year-old daughter about her budding sexuality.

In March 2016, after Polette ordered Valérie to undergo yet another sexual humiliation by a client, she killed him with a single bullet to the back of the neck while he was in the driver's seat, using a pistol he kept in the car. She wanted to ensure her daughter would not suffer the same fate that she had.

It shows she finally spoke up, if only for someone else.

The maternal instinct knows no bounds. It just is. The lengths to which some women will go in order to become a mother are extraordinary. So too is what they are willing to do, to risk, or to endure: multiple miscarriages, endless rounds of IVF, surrogacy, adoption, fostering, freezing eggs and sperm, donor insemination — almost anything to satiate the burning inner desire to become a mother.

Not to realize their need to have a child may release in a dominant Demeter archetype the shadow aspects of their personality, and lead to a sense of frustration and failure unless alternative means of assuaging the Mother and Nurturer archetypes within are found. This could be in the caring and healing professions — childcare, aged care, nursing, teaching, health and wellbeing — as well as in charitable or humanitarian organizations focused on helping the poor, disadvantaged, disabled, mentally ill, homeless or refugees.

Demeter archetypes are also at the heart of animal shelter and welfare work, rescuing and caring for pets and wildlife. Pets are often seen as babies or children. The desire to mother, to nurture, can be found in gardeners, farmers, landscapers, and also in the creative sphere — in artists, sculptors, writers, architects, even politicians.

The Mother is a universal power. We are all under the influence of the Mother archetype when we birth a project out into the world. Anyone who has a project or a life goal can embody Demeter by bringing their ideas and creations to life, by giving birth. Seeds, orchids, apples, pigs, parks, paintings, poems, books, homes, buildings or any kind of project can be viewed as progeny.

Frida Kahlo (1907–54)

Renowned Mexican painter Frida Kahlo embodies the universal power of the mother. Frida suffered polio as a child and a horrific bus accident as a teenager, in which a piece of handrail impaled her. The accident left her with multiple fractures of the spine, collarbone and ribs, a shattered pelvis, broken foot and a dislocated shoulder.

The terrible accident caused Frida to live her life in chronic pain. She needed frequent surgery for her spinal injuries and was largely confined to bed. It was in her bedridden state that Kahlo discovered a love for painting; the Demeter in her was deeply embedded, demanding to be freed. 'I am not sick. I am broken. But I am happy to be alive as long as I can paint.'

Life experience is a common theme in Frida's paintings, sketches and drawings. Her physical and emotional pain are depicted starkly on canvases, as is her turbulent relationship with her husband and fellow artist, Diego

Rivera, whom she married twice. To her, 'Diego was everything; my child, my lover, my universe'.

Frida was desperate to give Rivera a child, but several pregnancies were terminated as doctors feared for her life. Her paintings touched on female issues such as abortion, miscarriage, birth, breastfeeding and much more: things that were strictly taboo and never spoken of in public in those days, but which were at the heart of a Mother, Nurturer archetype. Frida's paintings, in essence, were her way of giving birth.

> Painting completed my life. I lost three children and a series of other things that would have fulfilled my horrible life. My painting took the place of all of this. I think work is the best.
> —Frida Kahlo

Other examples of Demeter

Mum Shirl, Angelina Jolie, Terri Irwin, Elton John

Reflections on the Demeter in you

Do you recognize the Goddess Demeter in you?

Is the Mother, Nurturer an archetype you strongly identify with?

How long has Demeter been in you?

List the ways Demeter manifests in you.

What gifts does the Demeter in you bring?

Any shadows?

Who are some other women who embody the Goddess?

9

Persephone

Goddess of Spring,
Queen of the Underworld

Archetype: Maiden

Vulnerability is the birthplace of love, belonging, joy,
courage, empathy and creativity. It is the source of
hope, empathy, accountability and authenticity. If we
want greater clarity in our purpose or deeper and more
meaningful spiritual lives, vulnerability is the path.

—Brené Brown, *Daring Greatly*

Persephone mythology

Persephone is the Greek Goddess of Spring and Queen of the Underworld. Her Roman name is Proserpina. Persephone was worshipped in two ways. As the only child of Demeter, Goddess of the Grain, Harvest and Fertility, and Zeus, King of the Olympians, she was also known as Kore, meaning daughter or maiden. Like Demeter, she was also a Goddess of Fertility.

In her other role as wife of Hades and Queen of the Underworld, Persephone was a more mature Goddess, possessor of the wisdom of the dark Underworld. Whenever the Greek heroes or heroines descended to the lower realm, Persephone was there to receive them. She and Hades also assisted souls who had just passed over and needed guidance to orientate and help them find their way.

Raised by her nurturing mother, Demeter, Persephone was a happy, carefree and compliant child, who gathered flowers and played with her stepsisters, her father's other daughters, the Goddesses Athena and Aphrodite. As signs of womanly beauty began to shine through her childlike innocence, the adolescent Goddess Persephone unconsciously attracted the attention of Hades, brother of Zeus and ruler of the Underworld.

One sunny day, Hades reached up from the Underworld as Persephone stooped to pick some wildflowers, abducted her, took her to his Underworld kingdom and made her his Queen. Although initially despairing and depressed, Persephone grew to love her husband and as Queen of the Underworld became one of the most powerful Olympian Goddesses.

Demeter scoured the Earth for her lost daughter. Because of her distress, she neglected the harvest and widespread famine ensued. Zeus then demanded his daughter be returned but, thanks to Hades' trickery, Persephone had eaten a few pomegranate seeds during her time in the Underworld. And anyone who tasted the food of the Underworld was condemned to remain there.

Zeus proposed a compromise: Persephone would spend half the year with her mother and half with her new husband. Thus, the seasons were born. Persephone spent six months below the Earth, during which time Demeter mourned. This period coincided with the dark winter months. However, when it was time for her daughter to return, Demeter brought back the light and the warmth and the Earth rejoiced. Persephone became the harbinger of spring, symbolizing growth and hope, and the renewal of life after death.

Persephone was usually depicted as a young Goddess holding sheafs of grain, a sceptre or a flaming torch, often in the company of her mother, Demeter. As Queen of the Underworld, she is depicted holding a pomegranate symbolizing her marriage to Hades and the Underworld.

Persephone archetype: Maiden (Damsel)

Persephone, the Goddess of Spring and Queen of the Underworld, is the Maiden, the archetype of the mother's daughter and the desire to be dependent. She is highly sensitive and receptive, and often perceived as eternally youthful and feminine. Unlike Hera and Demeter, who represent strong instinctual feelings and personalities, Persephone's archetypal patterns are much less distinctive.

A young Persephone may come across as passive, compliant, an easy-going child who never makes any trouble or causes confrontation; she is often indecisive and unsure what she wants to do when she grows up. But all that can change when a Persephone matures.

The older Persephone represents a more receptive and intuitive, sometimes spiritual woman who, when innocence is lost and family attachments are loosened, can begin to consciously ripen and create a life for herself.

Persephone belongs in the relational Goddess category, where her identity is dependent on her being in a significant relationship. She expresses a tendency towards passivity and the need to please and be wanted by others. In this way, Persephone's very close relationship with her mother, Demeter, made her vulnerable. Another aspect of her vulnerability was her pain and humiliation when abducted, taken to the Underworld and raped by Hades.

The closeness of Persephone to Demeter encouraged her to want to please her mother, to be a good girl. Being a good girl keeps a woman in her place, ensures she is well behaved, follows the rules and doesn't make waves. She only wants to stand out for the right things and definitely doesn't want to be singled out for doing something wrong. She blindly follows the path that's expected of her.

Sometimes the Maiden's relationship to her mother may be so close she is unable to develop an independent sense of self. She may stay sheltered in the shadow of her mother, Additionally, a mother may nurture her daughter's dependence in order to keep her close or to be an extension of herself, through whom she can live vicariously.

Sometimes it may be the adoring father who is too close, who brings up his daughter as Daddy's little girl or Daddy's little princess, surrounded by beauty, abundance and praise. Or, alternatively, either parent may become intrusive, over-controlling or abusive when the daughter tries to spread her wings.

Society often conditions girls to equate femininity with passive, dependent behaviour. In many cultures, the Persephone archetype's qualities, such as being attractive, youthful, attentive, receptive, quiet, adaptable and innocent, still determine how a perfect woman should be. This naive image of a woman's nature can cause great suffering to women for whom these qualities are not natural.

A relationship with a man or a woman can be the means through which a Persephone archetype separates from her mother or a dominating parent. She may leave home for good, severing the bonds entirely, or, like Persephone, share her time between her parents and her partner.

Sometimes a Persephone archetype may rebel and find herself drawn to risky situations and dark, abusive people; then she becomes a damsel in distress, the oldest popular archetype in literature and movies. The damsel is invariably beautiful, vulnerable and in need of rescue, either by a knight or a prince. The damsel awaits a suitor who is worthy of her beauty and rank, with whom she will fall madly in love and lead a charmed life.

When life disappoints, a Persephone archetype must learn ways to empower and take care of themselves. This archetype often matures after enduring significant emotional and/or physical abuse or loss. A Maiden or damsel may find their own strength and the beginning of their maturation in circumstances of extreme powerlessness, as did Persephone when she was abducted and raped.

As a captive in the Underworld, Persephone became depressed. The Underworld represents our unconscious, our repressed thoughts or feelings. When the darkness threatens to overwhelm or draw them down, people feel forsaken, and retreat to a place where there is no hope. Just a fathomless, black void.

The shadow side of Persephone archetypes mistakenly fosters patriarchal views that women are weak, helpless and in need of protection. This may lead a woman to expect someone will fight her battles for her while she remains devoted, beautiful and safely hidden away. Many women still expect to marry someone who will give them a home and take care of them. Correspondingly, some men are still raised with similar expectations.

> **Light:** youthful, attentive, receptive, intuitive, quiet, flexible, adaptable, innocent, energized, optimistic, creative, spiritual, inner strength

> **Shadow:** obedient, emotionally dependent, passive, compliant, diffident, people-pleasing, lack of autonomy, drawn into dangerous relationships

Persephone in others

Persephone is a vulnerable Goddess whose happiness, to a large extent, is determined by her relationships with others. The Maiden archetype often expresses a woman's compliance and passivity and the need to please and be wanted by others. Being abused or taken advantage of may cause the shadow aspects of her personality to overwhelm. Alternatively, it could become cause for empowerment.

Marilyn Monroe, Mary, Crown Princess of Denmark, Gwyneth Paltrow and her daughter Apple Martin, Whitney Wolfe Herd and Britney Spears personify a range of Persephones.

Marilyn Monroe (1926–62)

In 1946, when Norma Jeane Baker signed a contract with Twentieth Century Fox, she shed her name to become Hollywood actress, Marilyn Monroe. This stunningly beautiful Maiden was the embodiment of Persephone. She made sex feel innocent just by being her eternally youthful, girlish self. 'Give a girl the right pair of shoes,' she once said, 'and she'll conquer the world.'

But, trapped by a traumatic childhood and difficult past, Marilyn was a captive of the Underworld. Her father had walked out on her mother as soon as he found out she was pregnant. After Marilyn's birth her mother often spent time in a psychiatric institution, while Marilyn was passed between twelve different foster homes and an orphanage. Along with being constantly uprooted, she was frequently sexually abused by the men who were supposed to protect her, but she determined, 'I will not be punished for it or be whipped or be threatened or not be loved or sent to hell to burn'.

During her teenage years, Marilyn was staying with a family friend who tired of taking care of her and so married her off to the man living next door. Just sixteen, she agreed to the marriage partly to avoid being sent to foster care or an orphanage, but she soon tired of being a housewife. Modelling and acting held greater allure. This was the first of three marriages in her short life, all of which would end in divorce.

Marilyn's experiences of sexual abuse were paired with a turbulent love life, which made her increasingly vulnerable, as did the fact that Marilyn Monroe wasn't a real person; she was a carefully cultivated character created by the little girl who dreamed of becoming a movie star. 'It's all make believe, isn't it?'

With her voluptuous figure sheathed in curve-hugging dresses, her seductive antics, soft breathy voice and radiant smile, it was no wonder Marilyn, the glamorous sex symbol, gained popularity. At Hollywood parties she was surrounded by men, many of whom would make inappropriate advances. Although Marilyn had many affairs, and many with eminent and powerful men, happiness eluded her. Drugs became her salve.

Never forgetting the abandonment of her father, Marilyn naively looked to the men in her life for love and protection, but was always cruelly disappointed and mistreated. This Persephone never grew up. She remained the eternal girl on the footpath laughing as her skirt billowed up around her waist. Marilyn spent her life in vain looking for a prince to rescue her. Instead, she was doomed to remain captive forever in her own Underworld.

> Dogs never bite me. Just humans.
> —Marilyn Monroe

Mary, Crown Princess of Denmark (1972–)

Even today, the most pervasive and enduring fairytales, myths, cultural images and stereotypes for girls and young women are romantic and fanciful in nature; yet they are still cherished as a real-life goal for many women. Fulfilment of one's life path is often seen, literally and metaphorically, as being plucked from obscurity, finding one's prince or princess, falling in love, marrying, having children and living happily ever after in a palace.

For Australian public relations consultant, Mary Donaldson, it was a dream come true. 'I mean, every child at one stage dreams of being a prince or a princess.'

Like Persephone, Mary was a much-loved child. Growing up in Hobart, Tasmania, with her Scottish parents and three older siblings, childhood was a happy time. An avid athlete and student, she left university and went into marketing. A chance meeting at a Sydney bar one September night in 2000 between Mary and a handsome young man named Frederik was the beginning of their fairytale romance.

Over the next few years the two were often seen together, both in Australia and Denmark, but it wasn't until September 2003 that the palace announced their engagement. Assuming her new role and its accompanying status as a queen-in-waiting required compliance and sacrifice. She agreed to relinquish her Australian citizenship, convert from her Presbyterian faith to the Danish Lutheran Church, learn Danish and give up her rights to the couple's children in case of divorce.

Speaking on the balcony of Frederik VIII's Palace at Amalienborg for the first time with her fiancé, Mary said, 'Today is the first day of my new role. It is something that will evolve over time and I have much to learn and experience.'

In May 2004, Mary Donaldson walked down the aisle to become Mary, Crown Princess of Denmark. The couple now have four children. When the ageing monarch of Denmark, Queen Margarethe, dies, Crown Prince Frederik will become King of Denmark and Mary his queen consort.

Twenty-one years on, Princess Mary and Prince Frederik appear as happy as ever. Celebrating her husband's 50th birthday, Mary said, 'I am so happy that you swept me off my feet and that we dared to fall for each other, not just for a moment, but for life'.

Mary personifies the dual roles of Persephone. She embodies the happiness and sense of being wanted, as well as the satisfaction and fulfilment of one's purpose in life that can accompany both two particular stages in a woman's life, especially when she is loved: first as the Kore or young maiden, and later as the mature maiden, confident and assured in her role and status as princess.

> I am, more than anything else, happy.
>
> —Mary, Crown Princess of Denmark

Gwyneth Paltrow (1972–) and
Apple Martin (2004–)

American actress and Goop wellness mogul, Gwyneth Paltrow, and Apple Martin, her eighteen-year-old daughter with Coldplay frontman Chris Martin, each personify the Goddess Persephone, as well as embody the close relationship between Demeter and Persephone.

Of naming her daughter, Gwyneth said, 'When we were first pregnant, her daddy said, "If it's a girl I think her name should be Apple".' It sounded so sweet, and it conjured such a lovely picture for me, you know. Apples are so sweet and they're wholesome, and it's biblical.'

As Apple got older, there was an increasing similarity between mother and daughter. Now, Gwyneth has a total mini-me with Apple. Both are youthfully attractive with long blonde locks, slender svelte bodies, glowing skin and sweet smiles. They share the same fashion sense, borrow each other's clothes, bond over make-up and share beauty tips — and are exceptionally close. So it was no surprise when the actress-turned-lifestyle-guru recruited Apple to promote her brand's new line of Goop Glow health and beauty products on social media.

'Happy sweet sixteen my darling girl,' Gwyneth posted. 'You are the light of my heart; you are pure joy. You are wickedly intelligent and you have the best, most dry, most brilliant sense of humour. I have the best time being your mom.'

Having a teenage daughter also influenced Gwyneth's decision to become an early, crucial source in the ground-breaking *New York Times* investigation into the sexual crimes of Hollywood producer Harvey Weinstein, which helped catapult the #MeToo movement into the mainstream and eventually led to Weinstein's downfall, arrest and prosecution. Gwyneth, as a Demeter, wanted to protect her daughter Persephone but also, as a mature Persephone, she recognized her younger self's vulnerability and powerlessness and the need to take charge of her own life.

> I was really scared ... I think society had shown us only basically examples where women coming forward ended up not being advantageous for the woman, but I really felt like it was time.
> —Gwyneth Paltrow

Whitney Wolfe Herd (1989–)

American Bumble CEO and founder, Whitney Wolfe Herd, embodies both the younger and more mature aspects of the Maiden archetype. Since starting her company in 2014, Whitney has created her own commercial empire. The Bumble dating app has over 100 million subscribers worldwide. Whitney became the world's youngest self-made female billionaire at 31. What is less well known, though, is that she started her own company after multiple instances of abuse and harassment.

In her early twenties, after working on several apps, Whitney joined the development team for the dating app, Tinder. In 2012, she became a co founder and vice president of marketing. She was the inspiration behind the name of the app and credited with fuelling its popularity on university campuses and growing its user base.

Whitney resigned from Tinder in 2014 due to growing tensions with other company executives; soon after she filed a lawsuit against Tinder for sexual harassment. Whitney received more than US$1 million as a settlement, but as a result was subjected to further vile online abuse and hate.

It was not the first time Whitney had encountered toxic masculinity. During her high school years, she was in an emotionally abusive relationship with a boyfriend who made her feel worthless. Like Persephone, though, the experiences of darkness and despair forced her to look inside and grow. 'It showed me a very dark side of relationships, and it helped inform my understanding of what was wrong with gender dynamics,' she said in an interview with *Time* magazine.

Whitney started drafting a female-only social network centred around compliments and then cooperated with Andrey Andreev, the founder of Badoo, to develop a new female-friendly dating app. After moving to Austin to create a new life for herself, Whitney came up with the revolutionary idea for a female-focused dating app. 'What if women make the first move, send the first message?' she thought. 'And if they don't, the match disappears after 24 hours, like in Cinderella, the pumpkin and the carriage?'

And, thus, Bumble was born. The underworld of online dating world had found its queen.

> Everyone deals with trauma differently, and recovery is always a work in progress. But courage is contagious, and the more that people stand up and speak out against misogyny, the faster we can create the kind of world where we won't have to.
> —Whitney Wolfe Herd

Britney Spears (1981–)

American singer Britney Spears became a teenage pop sensation in the late 1990s. But the runaway success of the princess of pop became overshadowed by her tumultuous personal life, which came under intense public scrutiny.

Britney exemplifies how, when the positive aspects of Persephone's personality are exploited, darkness can overwhelm. And how the self-awareness of a more mature Persephone can finally sever the umbilical cord and help her fight her way back to the light. 'I was always a mama's girl growing up. I'm from the South, so there's always something about me when I'm just with my girls or even my mother. There's just a strong connection there.'

Britney started performing at the age of two. By age fifteen, she had made a demo tape which led to being signed by Jive Records. Releasing her first single, *Baby One More Time*, the song's lyrics were as controversial as her Lolita-like schoolgirl image in the video. The song quickly went to number one, as did the album of the same name, selling over 10 million copies in the United States. Her second and third albums were successful, too. But Britney still drew criticism for her revealing attire, which was copied by her multitude of young female fans. She claimed to be a sweet, innocent Southern girl at heart, but her image became progressively more sexualized. Britney countered, 'Just because I look sexy on the cover of *Rolling Stone* doesn't mean I'm naughty.'

Britney continued performing and making records, but often found herself in the spotlight more for events in her personal life than her music, in particular her tumultuous marriage to dancer Kevin Federline, and her increasingly erratic behaviour. This involved drinking, taking drugs, panty-less partying in Paris, her parenting style, property damage, traffic offences, rehab, shaving her head, and a brief admission to a psychiatric institution. This resulted in her being placed under a court-ordered conservatorship in 2008; with her father named as a conservator. Her legal, financial and sexual rights were denied her. 'He loved the control he had over me, one hundred thousand percent.'

Concerns about this arrangement later caused fans to start the 'Free Britney' online campaign. After enduring significant emotional trauma and loss, and now with greater self-awareness, a more mature Britney petitioned in 2021 for an end to the conservatorship. She claimed the arrangement was abusive and unnecessary, especially given that she was performing and recording. Later that year, a judge ruled in her favour and Britney's father was suspended as conservator. Persephone had grown up and reclaimed herself.

> I just want my life back. It's been thirteen years and it's enough. I truly believe this conservatorship is abusive.
> —Britney Spears

Other examples of Persephone

Audrey Hepburn, Patty Hearst, Rose McGowan, Taylor Swift

Reflections on the Persephone in you

Do you recognize the Goddess Persephone in you?

Is the Maiden archetype one you strongly identify with?

How long has Persephone been in you?

List the ways Persephone manifests in you.

What gifts does the Persephone in you bring?

Any shadows?

Who are some other women who embody the Goddess Persephone?

10

Aphrodite

Goddess of Love, Beauty and Desire

Archetype: Lover, Creative

Till I loved I never lived — enough
—Emily Dickinson

There is only one happiness in this life,
to love and be loved.
—George Sand

Aphrodite mythology

Aphrodite is the Greek Goddess of Love, Beauty and Desire. The Romans called her Venus. According to Hesiod's *Theogony*, Aphrodite rose from the white foam (*aphros*) produced when the severed genitals of her father, Uranus, God of the Sky, were thrown into the sea by his son, Cronus. She emerged as a beautiful, naked, fully developed woman who rode on a scallop shell.

Although also the Goddess of the sea and of seafaring, Aphrodite was known primarily as a Goddess of love. She presided over passion, pleasure, procreation and all aspects of sexuality, and has inspired more works of art than any other figure in classical mythology.

When Aphrodite first came ashore, she was escorted by Eros (Love) and Himeros (Desire) into the assembly of gods and was received as one of them. They were all struck with admiration and love when Aphrodite appeared; her surpassing beauty made every man desire her for his wife. Many gods believed that her beauty would create such competition for her hand that it could lead to a war of the Gods.

So Zeus married Aphrodite to Hephaestus, the God of the Fire and the Forge, who, because of his ugliness and deformity, wasn't seen as a threat. Hephaestus was happy to be married to the Goddess of Beauty, and forged her beautiful jewellery, including a magic golden girdle woven with the irresistible powers of love and desire. But the marriage was not a happy one, as he was often cuckolded by her.

Aphrodite's seductive charm had the power to ignite love and desire among Gods, mortals, even the birds and beasts; she personified the regenerative powers of nature. Aphrodite had many lovers, including Ares, the God of War, with whom she had three children, and the mortals Anchises and

Adonis. Priestesses served her in temples of love by making love with men as ritual offerings, as eros and procreation were considered holy. Any child born to the priestesses would belong to the Temple of Aphrodite.

But the wrath of the Goddess, when incited by those who scorned her love, made hubristic boasts or refused to honour her properly, was as legendary as her beauty. When the great Greek hero Heracles seduced her mortal lover Adonis, the Goddess retaliated by instructing the dying Nessus (a centaur whom Heracles had shot with a poisoned arrow) to have Deianeira, Heracles' wife, soak a robe in his poisoned blood and present it to her husband as a love charm. She did so, and brought about the hero's death.

Depicted as a beautiful, usually nude woman, the Goddess was often attended by a retinue of winged godlings, called Erotes, and associated with symbols such as the dolphin, dove, sparrow, swan, rose, sweet fragrances and fruit, especially the golden apple, the mirror and the scallop shell. Aphrodite was the personification of love, beauty and desire.

Aphrodite archetype: Lover, Creative

Aphrodite is a transformational or alchemical Goddess, as they are sometimes known. They are worshipped for their beauty, their magnetic personalities and their magical power to transform — themselves and others. Transformational Goddesses have the energy and synergy to touch deep chords, which can result in the birth of something new; often, in the case of Aphrodite archetypes, this can mean a new relationship or a work of art.

The Goddess of Love, Beauty and Desire is the archetype of the Lover. Her beauty and charm can entice mortals and deities to enter into illicit affairs, or to fall in love and conceive new life. Aphrodite inspired poetry and art and symbolizes the transformative and creative power of passion, love and sexuality.

The Aphrodite archetype governs a woman's passion and pleasure, and the joy that love, beauty, sexuality and sensuality can bring. She represents the feminine archetype of relationship and love; the uniting of feminine and masculine energies through sexual union. She is adored for her beauty, her alluring manner and her amorous adventures. The Lover archetype is exotic and erotic, a seductress who excites her lovers to passion. She feels rather than thinks and delights in emotion and unbridled passion with reckless abandon.

Every woman who loves and is loved in returned is transformed into a Goddess of Love. She feels beautiful, desired, sensual, sexually aroused — an archetypal Lover. Magic can happen. A mutual synergy is created; a magnetic attraction, an erotic enchantment, or an enhanced emotional electricity that can sweep people off their feet. But woe betide the person who falls in love with someone who does not return that love. Being rebuffed magnifies the intensity of hurt feelings and amplifies the sense of betrayal, cruelty, pain, longing and loss.

The Aphrodite archetype, though, is not attracted to permanent relationships as the relational or vulnerable Goddesses are. She falls in love often and easily. She seeks love because love is her conduit to beauty, desire, passion, pleasure, procreation and sometimes power and prestige. She has the power to disarm her lovers, to leave them vulnerable and open to the magic of eros between them. To consummate their union, to procreate, where new life may follow.

Aphrodite's divine gift is Eros, her divine son, the God of Love and leader of the Erotes, also known as Cupid. The Lover archetype admires powerful, potent, virile men. She feels comfortable with multiple relationships or extramarital affairs and, like the Goddess, is often attracted to younger men.

Typically, the Lover archetype is recognized for her mesmerizing beauty and physical attributes, but this is often not enough on its own. When combined with personal charisma and charm, and an innate sensuality, people are captured, almost unconsciously and against any natural reserve. Even when the Lover is the dominant archetype of a plain woman, it is often the warmth of her personality that charms and attracts.

Aphrodite's influence on relationships is not limited to romantic or sexual love. It can be a close friendship, platonic love, a soul or spiritual connection, some kind of compassion or understanding, or union of heart and mind that affects both people involved.

Aphrodite is also attracted to other creatives. Of course, this archetype may be expressed through sex or through the creative process, but the Creative archetype often inspires passion in others for seeking beauty, the arts and culture of all kinds. A creative spark is ignited, an alchemical reaction to her magnetic attraction where something fresh, new, brilliant or beautiful may emerge.

If Aphrodite is dominant in a Creative archetype she will be a force for change. Instead of serial lovers, it will be constantly evolving creative projects that fascinate her. It may be that her artistic ideas and creative energy create the magnetism and intensity that attracts admirers to her. Or, alternatively, Aphrodite will inspire other creatives — painters, writers, philosophers and poets — to abandon themselves and fall deeply in love, to embrace the intensity of their creative nature and spirituality, even if it leads to the risk of pain and heartbreak.

Some women, like the flamboyant rebel George Sand, one of France's best-selling writers, embody both the Lover and the Creative archetype. George was as well known for her troubled marriages and romances, her many affairs (often with fellow creatives — male and female) and excessive lifestyle as for her intellectual and artistic life and her prolific literary output of over 70 novels in her lifetime.

The Lover archetype often attracts guilt and judgmental attitudes, particularly in conservative patriarchal societies and religions. The Aphrodite archetype — the woman who incites passion and flaunts her sexuality and enjoys sex — is often associated with stereotypical notions of the whore and shame, which may induce the shadow side of Aphrodite to come to the surface.

But wherever and whenever Aphrodite is a part of a woman's psyche, chemistry can and will happen.

> We experience the alchemy of Aphrodite when we feel drawn to another person and fall in love; we feel it when we are touched by her power of transformation and creativity.
>
> —Jean Shinoda Bolen, *Goddesses in Everywoman*

Light: spontaneous, generous, charming, sensual, sexual, passionate, loving, emotional, erotic, spiritual, creative, wholehearted, beautiful, ravishing

Shadow: moody, selfish, melodramatic, obsessive, deceitful, excessive, hedonistic, indulgent, insatiable, vengeful, homewrecker, fatal attraction

Aphrodite in others

Vita Sackville West, Elizabeth Taylor, Brigitte Bardot, Rihanna and Lady Caroline Lamb personify the beauty and magnetic charm of Aphrodite. They are exotic and erotic, seductresses who symbolize the transformative and creative power of passion, love and sexuality. They feel rather than think, and delight in emotion and unbridled passion with reckless abandon, sometimes to the detriment of their own wellbeing or that of those closest to them.

Vita Sackville-West (1892–1962)

English author, poet and renowned gardener, Baroness Vita Sackville-West was the embodiment of Aphrodite. Vita was known for her exuberant aristocratic lifestyle, her passionate bisexual affairs (the most notable with novelist Virginia Woolf), her prolific writing and for the stunningly beautiful Sissinghurst Castle Garden, which she and her adored, also bisexual, husband Sir Harold Nicholson created at their estate in Kent.

Vita's passion for sex, writing, gardening and beauty was an unstoppable force that arose from the irresistible urges of the Lover and Creative archetypes within her, but which mocked the societal mores of the time. Vita and Harold's dual orientations never expected exclusive heterosexual passion from each other. Theirs seemed to be as much a spiritual union that ensured their many affairs never undermined their love, intimacy and their mutual creative chemistry and artistry.

In the 1930s Vita and Harold purchased and began the transformation of Sissinghurst Castle. The transformative nature of their union was epitomized in Harold's architectural planning and design of the garden rooms, complemented by Vita's colourful, abundant plantings. Their love was further reflected in the romance and intimacy of Vita's poems and writings.

The same sense of alchemy was apparent with Vita's affairs, especially with Virginia Woolf. Vita awoke in Virginia the kind of passionate sexuality and love she had never felt before. It was Harold who expected Virginia to open in Vita *a rich new vein of ore*, although they both feared that Virginia didn't possess the emotional resilience to withstand the intensity of Vita's seduction without her collapsing. Theirs proved to be a procreative love affair, resulting in a magical creativity and artistic outcomes for both women. Virginia's most successful book, *Orlando: A biography,* inspired by Vita's family history, is sometimes referred to as the longest and most charming love letter in history.

Happily, half a century after her death, the intoxicating effect of Aphrodite's passion and love in Vita live on, in her writing, her gardening vision at Sissinghurst, and in her prescient wisdom.

> The psychology of people like myself will be a matter of interest, and I believe it will be recognized that many more people of my type do exist than under the present-day system of hypocrisy is commonly admitted ... I do believe that their greater prevalence, and the spirit of candour which one hopes will spread with the progress of the world, will lead to their recognition.
>
> —Vita Sackville-West

Elizabeth Taylor (1932–2011)

English born Hollywood actress Elizabeth Taylor was Aphrodite incarnate, on screen and off. She had an insatiable appetite for the opposite sex. Married eight times (twice to Welsh actor Richard Burton), Elizabeth was a woman who knew how to live and love. She had the kind of love life and sex life that read more like one of her movie scripts than reality, and was honest about herself: 'I've always admitted that I'm ruled by my passions.'

At the outbreak of World War II, the Taylor family moved to California, with Elizabeth becoming a child star in films such as *National Velvet* and *Lassie*

Come Home. Sexually precocious and physically mature from an early age, the violet-eyed Elizabeth was in the public eye from the age of eleven and remained there for decades, long after her fame as a movie star waned.

Like Aphrodite, people were captivated by her incandescent beauty, her tantalizing screen presence, her sensuality and sexuality, her tumultuous love life and her eternal love affair with fine jewellery, especially diamonds. 'Big girls need big diamonds,' she once said, 'I adore wearing gems, but not because they are mine. You can't possess radiance; you can only admire it.'

Elizabeth embodied the Lover archetype. Enticed by her dazzling beauty, her magnetic presence and seductive charm, men swooned over her, adored her. She, in turn, fell in love easily and often, and out of love just as easily. Her first marriage at seventeen was a classic fairytale romance that lasted eight months. But longevity was never a feature of her relationships until she met the greatest love of her life, Richard Burton. They were equally besotted, passionate and tempestuous.

> She was unquestionably gorgeous. I can think of no other word to describe a combination of plenitude, frugality, abundance, tightness. She was lavish. She was a dark unyielding largesse. She was, in short, too bloody much.
> —Richard Burton (1925–84)

During this turbulent and stormy part of her life, Elizabeth's shadow side was in the ascendancy. 'When you are in love and lust like that,' she once said of her relationship with Burton, 'you just grab it with both hands and ride out the storm.' In spite of years of excess, extravagance, turmoil, scandal, alcohol, torrid love affairs, two fiery marriages, two tumultuous divorces and two subsequent marriages for Elizabeth, their love endured.

For 79 years this Goddess of Love, Beauty and Desire lived her life exactly as her heart dictated.

> Follow your passions, follow your heart,
> and the things you need will come.
> —Elizabeth Taylor

Brigitte Bardot (1934–)

Best known as the sex symbol of the 1950s and 1960s, Brigitte Bardot is a French model, singer, actor and animal rights activist. She broke all the stereotypes of her time, her life as epic as her fame and, like the drama of some of her films, Brigitte personifies Aphrodite.

Brigitte's ravishing beauty, erotic sexuality and nudity in the movie, *And God Created Women*, directed by Roger Vadim, created her sensational sex kitten persona and made her an international star. French writer and philosopher Simone de Beauvoir was so impressed with the young actress that she declared Brigitte the most liberated women of post-war France and wrote an essay titled *The Lolita Syndrome* about how men are attracted to younger women.

But the shadow side of Brigitte as sex symbol was more in evidence throughout her life than her light side. While Brigitte had many lovers, including women, and was married four times, she tried to kill herself at least four times. Her first suicide attempt was at sixteen when she had fallen in love with Roger Vadim, then a director's assistant. They began an intense affair but when her wealthy parents found out, they threatened to send her away to England. Then, when Brigitte tried to kill herself, her parents relented, permitting the relationship, but forbidding the couple from marrying until Brigitte was eighteen.

Brigitte was as intoxicated by the charismatic Vadim as he was with her. But, as he said, 'From the moment I liberated [Brigitte Bardot], the moment I showed her how to be truly herself, our marriage was all downhill. The only thing I love in love is all the feelings, the imaginations, the orgasms of the woman.'

Brigitte then married French actor Jacques Charrier but eschewed having children. In her memoirs, she describes her horror at finding herself pregnant aged 25. 'I looked at my flat, slender belly in the mirror like a dear friend upon whom I was about to close a coffin lid.' She revealed an attempt to abort the child, repeatedly punching herself in the stomach and referring to her unborn son as a cancerous tumour. On her 26th birthday, shortly after Nicolas was born, Brigitte tried to take her life again. The marriage ended soon after, with Charrier raising their son, and Brigitte declaring, 'I'm not made to be a mother. I'm not adult enough — I know it's horrible to have to admit that, but I'm not adult enough to take care of a child.'

After more suicide attempts, more lovers and more husbands, Brigitte turned her attentions to animal rights activism and in 1986 established a foundation to care for suffering animals. The Aphrodite archetype was no longer dominant.

> I gave my beauty and my youth to men. I am going to give my wisdom and experience to animals.
>
> —Brigitte Bardot

Rihanna (1988   )

Barbadian singer, actress, fashion designer and businesswoman, Robyn Rihanna Fenty, better known by her stage name Rihanna, is a modern-day Aphrodite who embodies the Creative archetype. She uses her beauty, talent, artistic ideas and creative output to create the magnetism and intensity to bring admirers to her.

Deeply affected by her parents' marital problems and her father's battle with drug and alcohol addictions, Rihanna turned to music as a teenager to escape her home troubles. At fifteen she met record producer Evan Rogers, on holiday in Barbados with his wife, who encouraged her to come to the United States. Soon after, Rhianna was signed by legendary rapper Jay-Z. By her third album, *Good Girl Gone Bad*, featuring *Umbrella*, the Grammy Award-winning hit single, Rihanna had undergone a total transformation from cute teen pop singer to a seductive, nubile woman with an abundance of erotic energy. She was now the ultimate superstar — a curvy, sultry siren who flaunted her sex symbol status in her next four albums, with songs with titles such as *Hard*, *Rude Boy*, *S&M*, all while revelling in her sexy and wild image. 'To me, sex is power,' she is noted as commenting. 'It's empowering when you do it because you want to do it.'

Renowned for her raunchy performances, music videos and barely-there stage outfits, Rihanna frequently tops the Sexiest Women Alive charts. She has been one of the most consistent hit makers in pop music with her chart-topping seven albums and collaborations with legends Jay-Z, Eminem, Kanye West and Calvin Harris, and winning countless awards.

Rihanna is very open and provocative about her sexuality, and isn't shy about sharing secrets about her fetishes, desires and bedroom antics. This modern-day Aphrodite is using her sex appeal to develop new creative outlets with brands such as Fenty Beauty and a lingerie collection, Savage Fenty, that includes a small selection of sex toys and accessories.

Rihanna is a Goddess calling aspiring Aphrodites to her temple of love, inspiring these priestesses to embrace their own love, beauty, desire, sensuality, sexuality, passion and pleasure, which in turn will entice lovers and admirers to worship and adore them.

> I want all women to feel great. We are women and
> we have challenges, we deserve to feel beautiful.
> —Rihanna

Lady Caroline Lamb (1785–1828)

English aristocrat Lady Caroline Lamb exemplified how the Lover and Creative archetypes can emerge later in life, often after the conventional chains of feminine societal expectations have been cast aside. Caroline illuminated how the shadow aspects of Aphrodite in her personality induced both a magnificent obsession and a fatal passion for the quixotic poet, Lord Byron.

Brought up in the eighteenth-century shadow of her parents' unhappy marriage and the unrestrained decadence of the Devonshire House set, Caroline was a fragile, agile and volatile child. She was unconventional, intense and highly temperamental in nature. She received no formal education and could not read or write until late adolescence.

At seventeen, Caroline was captivated by William Lamb who, after his elder brother died and his fortune changed, proposed marriage to her. (Lamb later went on to become Lord Melbourne and British prime minister.) They married, but William failed to live up to her romantic notion of what a lover should be and so, slowly, painfully, despite her husband's devotion, the marriage fell apart.

Caroline, a vivacious, flirtatious woman, a captivating conversationalist and now a passionate writer, decided the only way she'd find happiness and therefore solve her problems was to have an affair. She became obsessed with writer and poet Lord Byron, and pursued her sinfully romantic hero, summing him up after their first meeting in July 1813 as, 'Mad, bad and dangerous to know … That beautiful pale face is my fate.'

She became Byron's lover during her first great flush of literary and poetic success. The Aphrodite within her now finally unleashed, their frenzied affair turned into a sexual melodrama. Caroline and Byron were wild about each other, their relationship as literary as it was libidinous. Byron described her as, 'the cleverest most agreeable, absurd, amiable, perplexing, dangerous fascinating little being that lives now or ought to have lived 2000 years ago'.

Their affair was conducted very publicly, with Caroline cuckolding her husband as did Aphrodite with Hephaestus. Caroline and Byron were both passionately jealous for the other's attentions and talked of eloping. But within a few whirlwind months Byron, tired of Caroline's obsessive behaviour, wrote to end their relationship.

Caroline could not let him go. Byron was an obsession. Her wrath, like Aphrodite when scorned, was legendary, and is what history now mostly remembers her for. Caroline's love turned to anger and she swore to destroy Byron. She wrote to him endlessly, stalked him, kept turning up at his London rooms in various disguises, ceremonially burnt his gifts to her on a bonfire, as well as an effigy of Byron and sent him a bloody lock of her pubic hair.

Swinging from devastating bouts of depression to wild manic episodes, Caroline stopped eating and turned to self-harm. Seeing Byron at a ball for the first time since their relationship ended, Caroline broke a glass and started slashing her arms. Her sanity showed signs of collapse. Society shunned her. Her husband threatened to have her sent away.

In desperation, she unleashed the Creative within herself. *Glenarvon*, a Gothic tale of fashionable society, was published anonymously in1816 and met with instant success. But Caroline's authorship of this thinly veiled account of her relationship with Byron was an open secret and further scandal ensued. Her husband was devastated and swore he would never see her again, but later relented as she spiralled downwards.

The shadow side of Caroline's personality reigned supreme for the rest of her sad and sorry life.

> I possessed what is called the best of hearts — a dangerous possession, as it is generally accompanied by the strongest passions, and the weakest judgement.
> —Lady Caroline Lamb

Other examples of Aphrodite

Ursula Andress, Isabella Rossellini, Sharon Stone, Beyoncé

Reflections on the Aphrodite in you

Do you recognize the Goddess Aphrodite in you?

Is the Lover, Creative an archetype you strongly identify with?

How long has Aphrodite been in you?

List the ways Aphrodite manifests in you.

What gifts does the Aphrodite in you bring?

Any shadows?

Who are some other women who embody the Goddess Aphrodite?

11

∞

Psyche

Goddess of the Soul

Archetype: Heroine

The women I admire for their strength and grace did not get that way because shit worked out. They got that way because shit went wrong and they handled it. They handled it on a thousand different days, in a thousand different ways, but they handled it. Those women are my superheroes.

—Elizabeth Gilbert

Psyche mythology

Psyche was the Greek Goddess of the Soul and the wife of Eros, the God of Love. Their Roman counterparts were known as Psyche and Cupid.

According to Greek mythology, Psyche was a mortal princess with such exceptional beauty and grace, she was believed to be a goddess. People from all over the world clamoured to see her loveliness and charm for themselves. Yet Psyche did not marry anyone from her legions of admirers. She wanted to marry the man she would love with all her heart.

Aphrodite, the Goddess of Love, was angered that a mortal woman was so admired and turning away from her to worship Psyche. Jealously, she asked her son Eros, the God of Love, to poison mortal men's souls so that they no longer desired Psyche. However, when Eros laid eyes on Psyche, he was so mesmerized by her beauty he fell in love with her himself and carried her off to his palace.

In order to hide his true identity, Eros instructed Psyche never to look at his face. However, one night she crept into the room with a candle to gaze upon her husband while sleeping to find he was a beautiful young man. Eros, angered by her distrust, forsook her. Psyche searched everywhere for her lost love and eventually turned to Aphrodite for help.

Aphrodite commanded Psyche to perform a series of seemingly impossible tasks. Psyche's love for Eros was so strong that she accomplished the first two tasks easily. The third one, however, the hardest of all, was a trap. Psyche had to go to the Underworld (Hades) and bring back to Aphrodite Persephone's box with the elixir of beauty, but was ordered not to open the box. Inside, instead of the elixir, was Morpheus, the God of Sleep. But Aphrodite knew Psyche's curiosity would cause her to open the box.

Psyche opened the box and fell asleep. When Eros found out what had happened, he ran away from the palace and begged Zeus to save his beloved Psyche. Zeus granted Psyche the gift of immortality so that the two lovers could be together for eternity. Consequently, the couple were married in a ceremony attended by all the Gods.

Over time, Psyche became known as the Goddess of the Soul. She was depicted as a butterfly-winged woman entwined with her husband Eros, with the butterfly symbolizing the soul. Today, the myth of Psyche and Eros symbolizes true love and transformation.

Psyche archetype: Heroine

Psyche is a transformational Goddess. Transformational Goddesses represent the archetypes of celebration, change, metamorphosis and passion and are worshipped for their beauty. Psyche's journey from mortal to Goddess and becoming the wife of Eros is the archetype of the heroine.

There is a Heroine in every woman. It is that inner voice that tells you, 'You can do it', that urges you to push beyond your limits. To find the wherewithal to face any challenge that befalls you. To try something new. To go somewhere you have never been. To reveal your sexuality. To conquer the dark forces that threaten to overwhelm. Everyday heroines who dream of what could be and dare to make it happen.

The Heroine/Hero archetype is one of the most recognizable archetypes in literature, film, television and video games. Any compelling story has a heroine or hero of some sort, one which the media celebrates whether they are flawed, tragic, brave or even villainous. But there is a Heroine in every woman and every woman undergoes a Heroine's journey at some stage in her life, often over several journeys, and at various turning points in her life. A journey that will take her to the deepest and darkest recesses of her soul.

The Heroine/Hero represents an archetypal process of overcoming an obstacle to achieve a specific goal. In real life, the aim may be to write a book, gain a PhD, change careers, come out, build a house, cope with a failing business or bankruptcy, leave home, have a baby, manage a serious illness, recover from an addiction, leave an abusive situation, separate or divorce.

In myths, the Heroine/Hero's objective is often to find a treasure (such as a ring, golden egg or true love), save a princess, triumph over tragedy, or return with the elixir of life. Psychologically, these are metaphors for the task ahead.

> The hero's main feat is to overcome the monster of darkness: it is the long-hoped-for and expected triumph of consciousness over the unconscious.
>
> —Carl Jung, *Archetypes and the Collective Unconscious*

While Jung refers to this archetype as the Hero, I will refer to the Psyche archetype as the Heroine, although Psyche is more an archetypal process, an archetypal journey that the Heroine undertakes. And because women often follow a different path to personal development, transformation and self-actualization, I will refer to Maureen Murdock's *The Heroine's Journey: Woman's quest for wholeness* instead of the classic Joseph Campbell's *Hero with a Thousand Faces*.

> So many women having taken the hero's journey,
> only to find it personally empty and dangerous for
> humanity. Women emulated the male heroic journey
> because there were no other images to emulate.

—Maureen Murdock, *The Heroine's Journey*

Although not prescriptive, and not all are experienced equally powerfully, the ten stages encompassed in Murdock's *The Heroine's Journey* are:

1. Separation from the feminine: where women leave the nurturing shelter of the archetypal Mother behind. Some strike out in search of success and a sense of self or flee negative associations or situations.

2. Identification with the masculine: to flourish in a male-oriented world, successful women often emulate male behaviour by abandoning the domestic sphere, suppressing emotional displays and adopting male traits in the professional sphere.

3. The road of trials: the Heroine confronts challenges and obstacles; she survives trials, earns kudos and learns difficult skills.

4. The illusory boon of success: having overcome her trials, the Heroine attains a measure of success, a powerful title, position or wealth, but sometimes wonders when she will feel she has truly succeeded.

5. Awakening to spiritual emptiness: the Heroine senses there is more to life and starts paying attention to her inner voice.

6. Initiation and descent to the Goddess: the Heroine experiences the dark night of her soul; she must face her shadow, the things within herself that hold her back from what she truly needs.

7. Yearning to reconnect with the feminine: the Heroine may sever connections with people or organizations that compromise her spiritual growth. She turns to the creative pursuits to unify mind, spirit and body.

8. Healing the mother/daughter split: the Heroine reconnects with her roots and finds strength in the past. She emerges from the darkness with a deeper sense of self, able to nurture others and be nurtured by them. She reclaims the female aspects of her personality she once regarded as weak.

9. Healing the wounded masculine: having reoriented her concept of femininity, the Heroine must shed toxic perceptions of masculinity.

10. Integration of masculine and feminine: the Heroine has come full circle. Masculine and feminine traits are integrated in a union of ego and self. She is whole, capable of genuine love for others and is true to her nature.

Light: courageous, brave, confident, competitive, noble, humble, indomitable will, achievement, personal development, transformation

Shadow: hidden motivations, braggart, bully, coward, insecure, inflated opinion of self, arrogant, win at all costs, unable to acknowledge limitations

Psyche in Others

Lozen, Tina Turner, J.K. Rowling, Erin Brockovich and Cate McGregor are Heroines. They typify Psyche's strength, struggle and sacrifice, and embody her indomitable will, resilience, passion and determination to overcome every obstacle to achieve their goals, transform their lives and, in so doing, become a beacon in the lives of others.

Lozen (1840–89)

Lozen was a Native American warrior and Chiricahua Apache medicine woman. Sister of famous Apache chief Victorio, and ally to the famous Geronimo, Lozen was a skilled fighter and strategist on the battlefield, and highly proficient in medicinal matters.

Additionally, she was her people's spiritual leader. Her spiritual abilities enabled her to detect the movement of her enemies, and thus plan her strategies. Dubbed the Apache Joan of Arc, Lozen is a Heroine, albeit with a tragic trajectory.

As a child, Lozen demonstrated abilities well beyond her years. She became a medicine woman and warrior — a role not common among her people. As an adult, she often fought alongside her brother Victorio as his right hand in protecting their people from the US government, which was encroaching on their lands.

With her gift for strategy, her ability to ride and shoot, and her willingness to confront all challenges and obstacles, Lozen's talents became the stuff of legend. Whenever the Apache needed to know how to plan an attack, Lozen had a supernatural ability to predict where the enemy was and would often pray to the Apache's highest deity, Ussen, for guidance. This is why she is so often compared to her European counterpart, Joan of Arc.

The Chiricahua Apache suffered great hardships because of the US military's raids and invasions. Lozen's tribe were forced to move often for survival. Even during these attacks, she sacrificed everything to protect her community. One enduring legend is that she delivered a baby in the middle of the desert while the US cavalry was chasing after their tribe.

> Lozen is my right hand ... strong as a man, braver than most, and cunning in strategy, Lozen is a shield to her people.
> —Victorio

In 1870, Lozen and her people were driven from their tribal lands and relocated to the San Carlos Reservation from where, in 1877, they decided to escape. When back on their own lands they still had to fight to preserve their freedom. Soon after, they were moved on to another reservation. Nevertheless, Victorio, Lozen and the other Apache warriors continued their fight against their oppressors.

In 1880, after Victorio was killed in a battle, Lozen joined forces with Geronimo. She fought alongside him for six years until he surrendered to the government. Lozen was imprisoned at a military arsenal in Alabama where, tragically, she died of tuberculosis and was buried in an unmarked grave. However, stories of Lozen's bravery and ferociousness lived on in the memories of the Apache people and she was hailed as their heroine and honoured in their songs.

Tina Turner (1939–)

The queen of rock'n'roll, American-born singer, songwriter and actress Tina Turner underwent a classic Heroine's journey. Born Anna Mae Bullock, Tina had a rough family life. Her parents were poor sharecroppers who split up and left Tina and her sister to be raised by their grandmother. As a teen, Tina immersed herself in the St Louis rhythm and blues music scene.

Tina first met her husband-to-be, Ike Turner, at sixteen. Although not initially drawn to Ike romantically, she was drawn to his voice. Striking out in search of success and a sense of self, when Tina got up to sing his version of B.B. King's *You Know I Love You*, their musical bond was formed. With Ike drawn to her powerful voice, they became the Ike and Tina Turner Revue, a famous rhythm and blues duo, and performed together successfully for twenty years.

But behind the scenes, Ike had brutal control over Tina's personal and professional life. In her memoir, *My Love Story*, Tina describes the harrowing emotional, physical, sexual and financial abuse she experienced during their relationship. She describes how he would physically and sexually abuse her then force her to go out on stage and perform. And why, in her dark night of the soul, she attempted suicide in 1968. 'I was living a life of death,' she explained.

Tina finally left Ike in 1976, escaping from a Dallas hotel while they were on tour, and after she retaliated when he struck her during another brutal fight. In spite of ongoing intimidation, she filed for and was granted a divorce. Like Psyche, she refused to give in. Tina made the choice to be a survivor, to end her marriage, to fight for a better future.

She emerged from the darkness, reconnected with her musical roots, found the strength to heal herself and went on to create an even more brilliant and successful solo career. Shedding her toxic perceptions and experience of marriage, Tina remarried in 2013 to successful German music executive, Erwin Bach, revelling in the fact that, 'He shows me that true love doesn't require the dimming of my light so that he can shine'.

Like Psyche, the Goddess of rock'n'roll had finally found her true love. And a talent that rocked the music world.

J.K. Rowling (1965–)

Best-selling English author J.K. Rowling (Jo) grew up surrounded by books. Her Heroine's journey, her quest to become a writer, started at an early age.

'I lived for books. I was your basic common-or-garden bookworm, complete with freckles and National Health spectacles.'

In1990, while travelling on a train from Manchester to London King's Cross, Jo dreamt up the idea for Harry Potter. Then, over the next few years, she drafted an outline for all seven books of the series.

When Jo moved to northern Portugal to teach English as a foreign language, she took all her Harry Potter notes. There, she married and had a daughter, Jessica, in 1993. When the marriage ended later that year, Jo returned to the United Kingdom to live in Edinburgh and brought Jessica with her, as well as the first three chapters of *Harry Potter and the Philosopher's Stone*.

> We do not need magic to change the world, we carry all the power we need inside ourselves already: we have the power to imagine better.

Now a single mother struggling to get by, Jo still managed to write the first four Harry Potter books, often in cafés. She had some extraordinarily tough moments as a solo parent, and often wondered how she could survive. 'I have never been remotely ashamed of having been depressed. Never. What's to be ashamed of? I went through a really rough time and I am quite proud that I got out of that.'

Achieving international acclaim and fabulous wealth pales into insignificance beside what her daughter Jessica told her recently: 'I never knew we were poor. I just remember being happy.'

In Edinburgh, Jo trained as a teacher and began teaching in the city's schools but continued to write in every spare moment. Having completed the full manuscript of the first book, she sent the first three chapters of *Harry Potter and the Philosopher's Stone* to a number of literary agents. It was rejected by twelve different publishing houses before Bloomsbury wrote back asking to see the rest of it. She was delighted when Bloomsbury accepted it.

J.K. Rowling's indomitable will, resilience and creative determination to overcome every obstacle to achieve her goal embodies the Heroine archetype. And her archetypal journey is embedded in many of the characters in the *Harry Potter* series, especially her unlikely hero, Harry.

By imagining the incredible world of Hogwarts, J.K. Rowling captured the hearts and imaginations of hundreds of millions of children worldwide with heroines and heroes able to deliver us from despair and bring us magic, adventure, intrigue and fun. Children who aspire to be brave and heroic too, as is J.K. Rowling.

> It matters not what someone is born,
> but what they grow to be.
> —J.K. Rowling

Erin Brockovich (1960–)

Erin Brockovich is an American consumer advocate, environmental activist and legal clerk. In 2000, actress Julia Roberts starred in the Oscar-winning film *Erin Brockovich*, which showed how Erin's persistence uncovered an environmental scandal.

The real-life Erin is an unlikely Heroine. After being seriously injured in a traffic accident, Erin, a struggling single mother of three, hired lawyers Masry & Vititoe to represent her. While Erin won a small settlement she was out of work at the time, so Masry offered her a job at their law firm as a file clerk. It was while organizing papers on a real estate case that Erin first found medical records which led to the largest toxic tort injury settlement in US history, totalling US$333 million dollars in damages.

Despite her lack of legal education, Erin, along with attorney Ed Masry, was instrumental in building a case against Pacific Gas and Electric Company of California in 1993. Her mantra, 'If you follow your heart, if you listen to your gut, and if you extend your hand to help another, not for any agenda, but for the sake of humanity, you are going to find the truth.'

Since the lawsuit, Erin has continued to work as a consumer advocate and environmental activist. She uses her notoriety and success to encourage others to stand up and make a difference. and has written an aptly named best-seller, *Take It From Me: Life's a struggle but you can win.* Because of her dogged fighting spirit, and her continuing fight against environmental polluters, Erin has been hailed as a true American Heroine and has become a champion for countless women and men.

> She thrives on being the voice for those who don't know how to yell. She is a rebel. She is a fighter. She is a mother. She is a woman. She is you and me.
> —Erin Brockovich

Catherine McGregor (1956–)

Catherine (Cate) McGregor is a prominent Australian transgender writer, who underwent a harrowing Heroine's journey lasting nearly six decades before she was able to bring her world into balance.

Cate had misgivings about her gender from an early age but it was not until 1985, after a prolonged period of alcohol and drug abuse, that she recognized she was transgender.

Cate took her last alcoholic drink on 2 June 1990; at the same time, she consciously abstained from living as a female transsexual. However, the final onset of gender dysphoria brought to her to the brink of suicide.

Cate moved in tough, uncompromising male-dominated circles. She was talented, intellectually brilliant, a decorated soldier, and an exceptional cricketer and rugby player. Nonetheless, she felt that people discerned effeminacy and softness in her. She was painfully shy, gentle and a loner. But with alcohol she felt a man among men. To complicate her life even more, in 1995 and while still living as a man, Cate met her soulmate, the woman who became her wife. 'The idea of living as a woman was enthralling,' she said, 'but the fear of losing relationships — and my career — was too great.'

She realizes now she probably should have transitioned around the age of 25, but her devotion to her mother and her deeply inculcated, unconscious religious fear of eternal damnation forced her to deny her feelings. Without the sedating effects of drugs or alcohol, Cate often found life in its raw form intolerably painful. 'Living as a woman with that affected falsetto voice and ribald humour about tucking away the tackle? No way. I would rather die. And I nearly did.'

Following a crisis point in November 2011, Cate felt she had to commit to a path of transformation if she wanted to survive, but it was not until 2012 that she repudiated her assigned birth sex and completed gender reassignment surgery when she was in her early 60s. '[I chose] to run the gauntlet of ridicule, rejection and contempt in choosing to live the final portion of my life as a transsexual. In pursuing survival, I found myself.'

Even after transition, Cate's brother refused to recognize her as female. Her marriage to her wife broke down. They divorced in 2016 but still remain friends. The Heroine had come full circle.

> The feeling of harmony is enormous.
> —Catherine McGregor, *Untold Resilience*

Other examples of Psyche

Joan of Arc, Amelia Earheart, Valentina Tereshkova, Katherine Johnson

Reflections on the Psyche in you

Do you recognize the Goddess Psyche in you?

Is the Heroine an archetype you strongly identify with?

How long has Psyche been in you?

List the ways Psyche manifests in you.

What gifts does the Psyche in you bring?

Any shadows?

Who are some other women who embody the Goddess Psyche?

12

libertas

Goddess of Freedom

Archetype: Liberator

What a woman desires above all else is the power of
sovereignty, the right to exercise her own free will.

—Ethel Johnston Phelps, *Gawain and Lady Ragnell*

Libertas mythology

Libertas is the Roman Goddess of Freedom. Her Greek equivalent is Eleutheria, but Eleutheria was also an epithet for the Goddess Artemis. Libertas is a Goddess in her own right, and the personification of liberty.

Libertas symbolizes independence, freedom from restraint, and personal and societal freedoms. She is usually portrayed as a mature woman with a laurel wreath or a pileus (a conical felt cap given to freed slaves) and a rod (vindicta), which was used in the ceremonial act of manumission (release from slavery). When the master brought his slave before the magistrate, a rod was laid on the slave's shaved head. This was accompanied with certain formal words which declared that the slave was freed. The slave was then given a pileus. Throughout the ceremony, the master held the slave, and after he had been pronounced free, he turned him round and let him go. Interestingly, slaves were frequently called upon to take up arms with a promise of their liberty.

The Roman Republic was established in 509 BCE simultaneously with the creation of Libertas and is associated with the overthrow of the Tarquin kings. The Goddess of Freedom was honoured and worshipped by all freed women and men. Her first temple, located on Aventine Hill, was ordered by the Tribune, Tiberius Gracchus, and was dedicated in 238 BCE. There is smaller shrine to her located at Cicero's home on Palantine Hill, and a small statue of her inside the Roman Forum. As well, many Roman coins and seals of the time bear her image.

Libertas' likeness was used around the world to symbolize freedom. In 1886, France gifted the United States the Statue of Liberty as a symbol of freedom, liberty and justice everywhere. Originally named 'Liberty Enlightening the World', this Libertas statue in New York wears a crown of seven solar rays, which represent the seven continents and the seven seas. She holds the Flame of Freedom, or the Torch of Enlightenment, in her right hand, and her gown is remarkably similar to that worn by the original Roman Libertas. With her feet surrounded by broken chains, the Statue of Liberty is a symbol of light and liberty, of freedom from enslavement, tyrants and tyranny.

Libertas archetype: Liberator

Libertas, the Goddess of Freedom is a transformational or alchemical Goddess, as she is sometimes known. Transformational Goddesses represent the archetypes of change and metamorphosis. They often have a dream and are dedicated to making that dream come true. Above all, the Liberator archetype personifies freedom.

There are countless stories about the Liberator archetype throughout history. Often liberators are hailed as great military or political leaders who free an entire country or people from oppression and enslavement, like Mahatma Gandhi, Abraham Lincoln or Nelson Mandela, to name a few. Or great religious leaders, offering a promised land, peace, spiritual freedom or an end to suffering like Moses, Jesus, Muhammad or Buddha. They are the harbingers of liberty or peace for they spread a message of hope, freedom and the way forward to a more peaceful life based on equality.

> To be free is not merely to cast off one's chains, but to live in a way that respects and enhances the freedom of others.
> —Nelson Mandela

The Liberator archetype is not gender specific, yet patriarchal societies are more likely to celebrate masculine feats over feminine. But, just as heroines and heroes may undertake parallel journeys in differing ways, the same is true of female and male Liberator archetypes. Both may embrace the same ideals, but their perceptions of what these ideals mean and the manner with which they pursue their objectives may differ markedly.

The Liberator archetype believes in freedom and equality. She has a strong conviction to do what's right and to enable others to embrace their independence and forge their own path. She manifests intrepid, tenacious and purposeful action.

Liberators have a deep sense of justice and readily recognize inequality, but oppression has many faces. It may be in the form of a corrupt government, unfair laws, cruelty, control of others, or in less obvious forms like physical disease, low self-esteem, limiting beliefs, rigidity or general helplessness.

In everyday life, and on a smaller scale, Libertas lives in us all. She is that inner voice that says this is not right, and eggs you on to move beyond the societal and cultural chains that bind you and keep you in place. The Liberator archetype can be an invaluable ally to ordinary people to help free them or others from old, entrenched attitudes and beliefs. The target can be the tyranny of self-inflicted negative patterns, poor nutrition, destructive relationships or addictive behaviours that pervade the psyche and personality like an insidious invading army.

Liberator archetypes have the ability to draw out of themselves, and others, the natural inclination towards freedom. They believe freedom is a birthright; that longing to be free is a part of human nature; and that the human spirit cannot bear to be enslaved. A Liberator will fight for others' freedom, but is always conscious of her own constraints to avoid being trapped by her own thinking or behaviour. By freeing her own mind, she sees how to free her people.

Charisma is not a necessary prerequisite for someone with this archetype; however, the Liberator archetype, in its fullest expression, is often a powerful, charismatic, compelling and ruthless leadership force for good. Mostly, she is required to act alone, according to the dictates of her conscience, which means cultivating a deep sense of self-trust. She knows the consequences may be dire, but acts anyway.

The Liberator archetype is hopeful, optimistic, has the courage of her convictions, is willing to risk everything to help free others, and rarely accepts defeat. She is expansive in her beliefs and willing to take personal responsibility. For her, freedom without responsibility is oppression.

Shadow Liberators possess natural leadership qualities and the self-assurance of the liberator, but with darker intent. They are intolerant and insist everyone embraces their vision of freedom. They want to free others only to bring them under their authority and control.

Shadow Liberators assume they know what is best for others and are convinced others should follow them. Although they speak the language of freedom, their actions are actually those of a tyrant, for they force their will on others. Shadow Liberators do not trust others to make the right choices, so they dictate their actions.

The Liberator archetype isn't just about leading epic battles or revolutions — she also works on a personal level. Fears, illusions, dogmas and dependencies are born of ignorance, and can hold you captive. The Liberator inspires others to become educated, to see the truth, to expand their awareness beyond the barriers of an oppressive relationship or system.

The Liberator archetype values free will above all else. She honours the choices of others and helps them to see the truth that helps them on the road to both outer and inner freedom. The Liberator treats her former oppressors with the same compassion and dignity as those who suffered beside her. She endeavours to live her life in a manner befitting her vision of a free, equal and just society.

Light: visionary, idealistic, charismatic, powerful, compelling, courageous, just, hopeful, open, expansive, self-trust, self-responsibility, belief in and willing to fight for education, equality or freedom

Shadow: self-righteous, autocratic, controlling, despotic, oppressive, ruthless, unjust, cruel, brutal, forceful, arrogant, destructive, disregard for others, violent, vengeful, believes the end always justifies the means

Libertas in others

Emmeline Pankhurst, Rosa Parks, Aung San Suu Kyi, Ruth Bader Ginsburg and Malala Yousafzai embody the Goddess of Freedom. They are leaders with a willingness to pursue purposeful action to achieve their aims, in spite of any personal hardship, suffering or threats. And all these Liberators, except Aung San Suu Kyi, remained true to their purpose in life.

Emmeline Pankhurst (1858–1928)

Emmeline Pankhurst personifies Libertas. She was a British political activist and militant champion of women's suffrage. Emmeline organized the British suffragette movement and led a successful 40-year campaign to enfranchise British women. 'It is right for women to fight for their freedom and the freedom of the children they bear.'

Seen as the face of the women's suffragette movement, Emmeline created the Women's Franchise League in 1889. The league wanted to enfranchise all women, married and unmarried alike, as some groups only sought the vote for single women and widows. However, lack of government action meant their voices went unheard. So, in 1903, Emmeline and her oldest daughter, Christabel, founded a new women-only group focused solely on voting rights, the Women's Social and Political Union (WSPU). Their slogan was, 'Deeds not words'.

The Women's Social and Political Union was a more militant group, using drastic activism, social unrest and civil disobedience to get their message heard. This included window-breaking, vandalizing public art and arson. However, this notoriously illegal action led to arrest and sometimes violence. 'We were called militant, and we were quite willing to accept the name. We were determined to press this question of the enfranchisement of women to the point where we were no longer to be ignored by the politicians.'

At times, the increasingly bitter skirmishes between the suffragettes and police bordered on warfare. Police and politicians, outraged by what they saw as 'hysterical women', demanded stronger action. More and more women were being arrested, including Emmeline. After arrest, the women would stage a hunger strike which resulted in them being force-fed.

In 1913, after the *Cat and Mouse Act* was passed, hunger-striking prisoners were released until they were well enough to be re-arrested. In the year following, Emmeline was imprisoned, released, then rearrested twelve times.

With the outbreak of World War I in 1914, Emmeline called off the campaign and committed the WSPU to the war effort, and the government released all suffragette prisoners. Emmeline instead turned her energies to supporting the war effort. In 1918, the *Representation of the People Act* was passed, enfranchising women over 30.

Emmeline died on 14 June 1928. Shortly afterwards, women were granted equal voting rights with men at age 21. The Goddess of Freedom's dream was finally realized.

> Women are very slow to rouse, but once they are aroused, once they are determined, nothing on Earth and nothing in heaven will make women give way; it is impossible.
> —Emmeline Pankhurst

Rosa Parks (1913–2005)

Rosa Parks was an African American civil rights activist whose refusal to give up her seat to a white man on a public bus was the spark that ignited the civil rights movement in the 1960s. 'I knew someone had to take the first step and I made up my mind not to move.'

Growing up in the segregated South, Rosa was frequently confronted with racial discrimination and violence. The viciously racist Ku Klux Klan was a constant threat and nights were particularly dangerous for Black people. Rosa's grandfather would often keep watch, rifle in hand, awaiting a mob of violent white men, windows and doors of the house boarded up, with the family crouched inside. Sometimes Rosa kept watch with her grandfather.

Rosa was active in the civil rights movement from a young age. At nineteen she married fellow activist Raymond Parks. Together the couple worked with many social justice organizations, believing, 'Each person must live their life as a model for others'.

On 1 December 1955, Rosa was on a bus in Montgomery when the driver asked Black passengers to stand in order to let white passengers sit. Three passengers stood, but Rosa refused and was arrested and fined. 'I have learned over the years that when one's mind is made up, this diminishes fear; knowing what must be done does away with fear.'

Rosa's actions inspired the leaders of the local Black community to organize the Montgomery bus boycott in Alabama. The boycott lasted more than a year, with protests taking place all over the United States.

On 13 November 1956, the US Supreme Court upheld a lower court's decision declaring Montgomery's segregated bus seating unconstitutional, and a court order to integrate the buses was served on 20 December. The boycott ended the following day.

After the boycott, Rosa and her husband moved around the country before permanently settling in Detroit, Michigan. There she was an active member of Detroit's civil rights movement and several organizations working to end inequality in the city. This Goddess of Freedom died at age of 92, leaving behind a rich legacy of resistance against racial discrimination and injustice. She became known as the mother of the civil rights movement.

> I would like to be remembered as a person who wanted to be free ... so other people would be also free.
> —Rosa Parks

Aung San Suu Kyi (1945–)

Aung San Suu Kyi, daughter of assassinated Burmese independence hero General Aung San, has spent much of her life overseas. Returning home in 1988 to Myanmar (previously Burma) to nurse her dying mother, Aung San Suu Kyi joined the student-led revolution against the military junta that had seized power after her father's death. She was a Libertas trying to free people from an oppressive regime, who believed that, 'Freedom and democracy are eternal dreams'.

Although softly spoken, Aung San Suu Kyi's passion for democracy was clear. She quickly rose to become the movement's outspoken leader, calling for free elections, respect for human rights and the reestablishment of democracy. When the National League for Democracy (NLD) won the next election in 1990, the military did not allow it to take office and many of its members, including Aung San Suu Kyi, were detained. Given the opportunity to leave the country, she declined, fearing she would not be allowed back. She spent nearly fifteen years under house arrest in her family's lakeside home but continued to fight for freedom.

In giving up her own freedom, Aung San Suu Kyi was hailed internationally as a vibrant symbol of resistance to authoritarian rule. In 1991, while still under house arrest, she was awarded the Nobel Peace Prize and hailed as an outstanding example of the power of the powerless. 'All people need freedom and safety to be able to realize their full potential.'

In 2015, after Aung San Suu Kyi's NLD party won the first free and fair election in decades, rules in the constitution prevented her from becoming president because her late husband and children were foreign citizens, so a special role of State Counsellor was created for her. She was seen as a revered leader, both at home and abroad. But when Aung San Suu Kyi failed to intervene in the rape, murder, atrocities and crisis that befell Myanmar's mostly Muslim Rohingya minority in 2016 and 2017, she was reviled by many. She was silent when the Rohingya genocide, a series of ongoing persecutions by the Myanmar military towards the Muslim people, forced over a million Rohingya to flee to other countries.

Aung San Suu Kyi publicly backed the military's crackdown on the Rohingya Muslim minority during her appearance at the International Court of Justice in 2019, saying the mass displacement of Rohingyas was due to an internal armed conflict. This led to a spectacular fall from grace in the eyes of the world. The Liberator had now become an oppressor.

As a result of its actions, Myanmar now faces a lawsuit accusing it of genocide at the International Court of Justice, while the International Criminal Court is investigating the country for crimes against humanity.

Aung San Suu Kyi was deposed by a military coup in 2021. Despite widespread criticism of her failure to protect the Rohingya people, to many of Myanmar's people she was still Mother Suu, so when news of her arrest by the military spread, a familial type of anger, shock, surprise, sadness and fear spread. Myanmar's mother was in trouble. She has said, 'It is not power that corrupts but fear. Fear of losing power corrupts those who wield it and fear of the scourge of power corrupts those who are subject to it.'

Aung San Suu Kyi remains enormously popular within her country and enjoys a level of adoration that other world leaders can only dream of. But she and the world are more aware of her shortcomings. It is unlikely that Aung San Suu Kyi will ever be hailed as a beacon for human rights by the international community again, but the inspirational words of this flawed and fallible Goddess of Freedom will live on.

> Freedom must be demanded and defended by those who have been denied it and by those who are already free.
> —Aung San Suu Kyi

Ruth Bader Ginsburg (1933–2020)

Ruth Bader Ginsburg was a US Supreme Court justice, serving from 1993 to 2020. After graduating in 1959, Ruth became a stalwart courtroom advocate for the fair treatment of women.

Like Libertas, Ruth always had a strong conviction about doing what was right and leading the way. Her life was committed to intrepid, tenacious and purposeful action to achieve gender equality for herself and for others, and the belief that, 'Real change, enduring change, happens one step at a time'.

Despite excelling academically, Ruth continued to encounter gender discrimination while seeking employment after graduation, but gradually she worked at breaking down barriers. She became the first female member of the prestigious *Harvard Law Review*; she co-founded the first law journal on women's rights and became the first female tenured professor at Columbia Law School. 'Women belong in all the places where decisions are being made,' she said. 'It shouldn't be that women are the exception.'

During the 1970s, Ruth co-founded and served as the director of the Women's Rights Project of the American Civil Liberties Union, for which she argued six landmark cases on gender equality before the US Supreme Court, five of which were successful. Ruth believed that the law was gender-blind and all groups were entitled to equal rights. 'Women will only have true equality when men share with them the responsibility of bringing up the next generation.'

As a judge, Ginsburg favoured caution, moderation and restraint. She was considered part of the Supreme Court's moderate-liberal bloc, presenting a strong voice in favour of gender equality, the rights of women and workers, and the separation of church and state. More recently, she was part of a critical ruling in favour of the *Affordable Care Act*, and the historic decision that made same-sex marriage legal in all 50 states.

Ruth's modus operandi was, 'Fight for the things that you care about, but do it in a way that will lead others to join you'. Embraced as a courageous feminist icon in the pursuit of social justice and gender equality, Ruth embodied the Goddess of Freedom. Her life and work were celebrated in the biography *The Notorious RBG* and in the 2018 film, *On the Basis of Sex*.

> I ask no favour for my sex. All I ask of our brethren
> is that they take their feet off our necks.
> —Ruth Bader Ginsburg

Malala Yousafzai (1997–)

In 2014, seventeen-year-old Pakistani human rights activist Malala Yousafzai became the youngest-ever Nobel laureate

Born in a country where welcoming a baby girl is not always cause for celebration, her father was nonetheless determined to give his daughter every opportunity a boy would have. Malala loved school, but when the Taliban took control everything changed. The extremists banned many liberties, decreed girls could no longer go to school and dealt harsh punishments for those who disobeyed.

Malala began her activism when young. At eleven, the young Liberator, aware of what women needed to flourish in a male-oriented world, began publishing a blog about her life in Taliban-occupied Swat Valley, and speaking out on behalf of girls and their right to learn. As Malala's story gained attention, she appeared in more publications and on television, where she shed light on Taliban oppression. This made her a Taliban target.

In October 2012, on her way home from school, a masked gunman boarded the school bus, asked, 'Who is Malala?' then shot her in the head. She woke ten days later in hospital in Birmingham, England. Doctors and nurses told her about the attack and how people around the world were praying for her recovery. The attempt on her life only strengthened Malala's resolve.

> It was then I knew I had a choice: I could live a quiet life or I could make the most of this new life I had been given. I determined to continue my fight until every girl could go to school.

Malala released her book, *I Am Malala*, in the year following the attack, and in 2014 was co-recipient of the Nobel Peace Prize, making her the youngest Nobel laureate in history. Not content with this measure of personal success, Malala and her father established the Malala Fund, a charity dedicated to giving every girl an opportunity to choose her own future. The fund is committed to providing free, quality primary and secondary education for every child by 2030. Malala believes that every girl has a right to education and that her vision can be achieved by world leaders divesting government funding from weapons and conflicts and instead investing them in books, education and hope. 'Let us remember: one book, one pen, one child, and one teacher can change the world.'

Malala travels to many countries to meet girls fighting poverty, wars, child marriage and gender discrimination so that they can to go to school and be educated. Although she was hailed as a global heroine after the attack, in her eyes the journey is far from complete. But this Goddess of Freedom uses her own torch to shine the way.

> I truly believe the only way we can create
> global peace is through educating not only
> our minds, but our hearts and souls.
>
> —Malala Yousafzal

Other Examples of Libertas

Virginia Woolf, Simone de Beauvoir, Amani Al-Khatahtbch, Nelson
Mandela

Reflections on the Libertas in you

Do you recognize the Goddess Libertas in you?

Is the Liberator an archetype you strongly identify
with?

How long has Libertas been in you?

List the ways Libertas manifests in you.

What gifts does the Libertas in you bring?

Any shadows?

Who are some other women who embody the Goddess
Libertas?

13

The twelve Goddesses in you

Bliss and joy come in moments of living our highest truth — moments when what we do is consistent with our archetypal depths. It's when we are most authentic and trusting, and feel that whatever we are doing, which can be quite ordinary, is nonetheless sacred.

—Jean Shinoda Bolen, *Gods in Everyman*

In introducing you to twelve Goddesses, their corresponding archetypes and 60 women who embody these Goddesses, *Goddesses in You* has presented you with a mirror into your own soul and into the lives of other women, in order to better understand yourself and others.

The potential of all these Goddesses is present in you, and in every woman. You are not limited to one Goddess or one archetype. You are all of them at some time in your life; you draw from them all. Some Goddesses are more dominant than others, but each of them is a gift to you. To fully embody your Goddess essence, the key consideration is whether or not she feels authentic.

These twelve Goddesses encompass the whole woman, the fullness of femininity, and represent our instincts and deepest desires. There are the elemental Goddesses who embody the powers of nature, elemental forces that reflect aspects of the natural world like the Earth, moon and sun. Then there are the independent Goddesses who represent the element of self-sufficiency and autonomy in the female psyche, who exist in their own right.

There are also the relational Goddesses who represent the traditional roles of women that depend on them being in a significant relationship, and have the potential to become problematic. And finally, the transformational Goddesses who represent change, metamorphosis, passion and wholeness and encourage us to surrender to the power of flow.

Goddess archetypes are female personality types that we intuitively recognize in ourselves, the women in our lives and in our culture. There is nothing inherently good or bad about a particular Goddess or personality type. Each Goddess archetype has both positive and negative traits.

You will be aware of the light and shadow aspects of these Goddesses in yourself. You will also be aware of these traits from the profiles of the women in the book or be reminded of others in your life. You might also recognize that shadow qualities have the potential to become symptomatic of illness or disease and/or cause problems or difficulties for yourself or others. What is important to understand is that your shadow's defence mechanisms, the intensity and type of emotions and behaviours exhibited, are all clues as to whether you are being true to your nature. The same is true for others.

It is important to reiterate that women are shaped by both inner and outer forces. These inner forces relate to the Goddesses and archetypal patterns that are imprinted on us, our DNA. The outer influences are more familial, societal, cultural or religious, and often come in the form of norms and stereotypes. A stereotype is harmful when it limits a woman's ability to develop her potential or to make choices about her life and life plans. The key is to be aware of your own instincts and desires and any conflicting priorities and commitments, and to consciously choose what is most important to you. To be true to yourself, and reject expectations or roles imposed by others. When there is synchronicity between who we are and what we do, joy and bliss abound.

By becoming conscious of, and connecting with, your Goddess or Goddesses, their archetypal patterns and the powerful influence they have on your psyche, you will discover the key to the real you, to your reality.

Goddesses and archetypes in you

The Goddess and archetypal wheel is a handy visual guide and reference to the twelve Goddesses and their feminine archetypes.

!

Reflections on the Goddesses in you

And now we have come full circle, back to the questions I posed in the introduction:

Who are you?

Which Goddesses do you recognize in you?

What makes up your personality?

Which Goddesses are/were more influential?

When and why?

At the deepest level, what instinctively drives you?

Which archetypes do you embody?

What gifts do the Goddesses in you bring?

What stereotypical gender roles are expected of you?

Any shadows?

Are you living the life of your true self?

Is there synchronicity between who you are and what you do?

Any shadows?

How has *Goddesses in You* helped you understand your life story?

How has awareness of the myths and archetypal patterns, as expressed in others, helped you to interpret the life stories of those closer to you?

Acknowledgments

Writing is often a very solitary and lonely process, but with *Goddesses in You*, I was blessed with two guardian Goddesses who were there for me.

Gaia, the Supreme Creator, in the guise of Gareth St John Thomas, CEO and publisher Exisle Publishing, and my marvellous mentor. Gareth welcomed me into his literary universe; he was there from the conception of *Goddesses in You* and throughout its gestation. Drawing on his powerful insights, wisdom and vast experience, Gareth nurtured me, guided me, challenged me and helped give birth to the beautiful book in me. What a precious gift!

Athena, personified by my dear friend, editor, wise woman and warrior, Dr Kim Murray. Kimmy dedicated her time, love and literary prowess to ensuring that the writing in *Goddesses in You* reflected reason, intelligence, clarity, wisdom and a touch of class. Just like her.

Thanks also to the talented team at Exisle, headed by publisher Anouska Jones, for giving life and form and beauty to the book.

Exisle Academy's mentoring program is an investment in the future of books and writers. It empowers writers to negotiate the publishing jungle by providing insider information about publishing that is rarely available in any other context.

And finally, to the beautiful Bella, my precious poodle, for her love, devotion and nearness, always.

References

Books

Allende, I. 2021, *The Soul of a Woman*, Random House, New York.

Baird, J. 2020, *Phosphorescence: On awe, wonder and things that sustain you when the world goes dark*, HarperCollins, Sydney.

Blackie, S. 2016, *If Women Rose Rooted: The journey to authenticity and belonging*, September Publishing, Tewkesbury, England.

Campbell, J. 2004, *Pathways to Bliss: Mythology and personal transformation*, New World Library, California.

Campbell, J. 1993, *The Hero with a Thousand Faces,* Fontana Press, London.

Future Women, 2020, *Untold Resilience: Stories of courage, survival, and love from women who have gone before*, Penguin Life, Sydney.

Greer, G. 2008, *The Female Eunuch*, Harper Perennial Modern Classics, London.

Greer, G. 2014, *White Beech: The rainforest years*, Bloomsbury Publishing PLC, Sydney.

Jung, C. 1989, *Memories, Dreams, Reflections*, Vintage, London.

Jung, C. 1991, *The Archetypes and the Collective Unconscious*, Routledge, London.

Lancewood, M. 2018, *Woman in the Wilderness: A story of survival, love & self-discovery in the wilderness*, Allen & Unwin, Sydney.

Murdock, M. 1990, *The Heroine's Journey: Woman's quest for wholeness,* Shambhala, Colorado.

Myss, C. 2013, *Archetypes: Who are you?* Hay House, Sydney.

Pinkola Estés, C. 1992, *Women Who Run with the Wolves: Contacting the power of the wild woman*, Rider, London.

Shinoda Bolen, J. 1984, *Goddesses in Everywoman: Powerful archetypes in women's lives*, Harper and Row, California.

Online references

ABC News, 3 July 2020, 'What do we know about Ghislaine Maxwell, Jeffrey Epstein's alleged accomplice who's been arrested by the FBI?': www.abc.net.au/news/2020-07-03/who-is-ghislaine-maxwell-connection-to-jeffrey-epstein/12419116

American Rhetoric, 10 October 2007, https://www.americanrhetoric.com/speeches/marionjonesapologyforsteroiduse.htm

The Australian, 24 April 2021: 'Rosie Batty: Happy times are more often than sad times now': https://www.theaustralian.com.au/weekend-australian-magazine/rosie-batty-happy-times-are-more-often-than-sad-times-now/news-story/dc700f800542172dfe2dd630b249bc39

Caroline Myss, Appendix A: A gallery of archetypes: https://www.myss.com/free-resources/sacred-contracts-and-your-archetypes/appendix-a-gallery-of-archtypes/

The Conversation, 9 October 2020, '*The Female Eunuch at 50*, Germaine Greer's fearless, feminist masterpiece': https://theconversation.com/friday-essay-the-female-eunuch-at-50-germaine-greers-fearless-feminist-masterpiece-147437

Erin Brockovich: my story: https://www.brockovich.com/my-story/

Frida Kahlo: www.fridakahlo.org

Grunge: www.grunge.com/644253/brigitte-bardots-tragic-real-life-story/

The Guardian, 21 June 2021, 'Woman to stand trial in France for killing stepfather after years of abuse': https://newsconcerns.com/woman-to-stand-trial-in-france-for-killing-stepfather-after-years-of-abuse-france/

Harpers Bazaar, 30 November 2017, 'You reported sexual harassment, now what? Bumble's Whitney Wolfe Herd offers advice': https://medium.com/harpers-bazaar/you-reported-sexual-harassment-now-what-bumbles-whitney-wolfe-herd-offers-advice-653036a400a8

HuffPost, 18 August 2017, 'Ellen DeGeneres's post for Portia is really freakin' sweet': https://www.huffpost.com/entry/ellen-degeneres-anniversary-post-for-portia-is-really-freakin-sweet_n_5995d8d0e4b0c8cc855bf531

HuffPost, 7 October 2018, 'Feminists' who exclude trans women aren't feminists at all': https://www.huffpost.com/entry/opinion-tannehill-terfs-right-wing_n_5b44eeeae4b0c523e2637878

Irish Times, 5 June 2003, 'Hillary's memoir spills the beans: "I wanted to wring Bill's neck"': https://www.irishtimes.com/news/hillary-s-memoir-spills-the-beans-i-wanted-to-wring-bill-s-neck-1.361465

Jane Goodall Institute UK: https://www.janegoodall.org.uk/jane-goodall/biography

Malala Yousafzai: https://www.malala.org/malala's-story

Nigella Lawson: https://nigella.com/books/how-to-be-a-domestic-goddess

Poetry Foundation, Emily Dickinson: https://www.poetryfoundation.org/poets/emily-dickinson

J.K. Rowling: https://www.jkrowling.com/about

The Royal Family: https://www.royal.uk/her-majesty-the-queen

WIO News, 7 September 2019, 'Gwyneth Paltrow reveals what motivated her to come forward about Harvey Weinstein': www.wionews.com/entertainment/gwyneth-paltrow-reveals-what-motivated-her-to-come-forward-about-harvey-weinstein-252356

Working with Indigenous Australians: http://www.workingwithindigenousaustralians.info/content/Culture3

General websites

Archetypal Nature: www.archetypalnature.com

Biography: www.biography.com

Biography Online: www.biographyonline.net

Ducksters: www.ducksters.com/biography/

Education — National Women's History Museum: womenshistory.org/education

Encyclopedia Britannica: www.britannica.com

Famous People in the World: www.thefamouspeople.com/

FemBio: www.fembio.org/

Forbes: www.forbes.com

Goddess Ceremony: www.goddessceremony.com

Goddess Gift: https://goddessgift.com

Goddess Guide: www.goddess-guide.com/

Greek News: https://greekcitytimes.com/

Greek Legends and Myths: www.greeklegendsandmyths.com/

Greek Mythology: www.greekmythology.com/

History BBC: https://bbc.co.uk/history

Know Your Archetypes: https://knowyourarchetypes.com/

Theoi Greek Mythology: www.theoi.com/

The Royal Forums: https://theroyalforums.com

Verywell Mind: www.verywellmind.com

Wikipedia: https://en.wikipedia.org/wiki/Main_Page

World History Encyclopedia: https://www.worldhistory.org/

Index